MONEY

Ancient Italian
bronze coin of
the city of
Hatra, 3rd
century B.C.

Australian
cupro-nickel 50 cents, 1970

Bolivian gold
8-scudos coin, 1841

Indian gold
"pagodas",
17th–19th century

Indian gold mohur,
17th century

Ceylon (Sri Lanka)
10-cent note, 1942

Djibouti French
colonial note,
20th century

Ancient Roman medals
showing minting
(below) and banking
(right)

Ancient Greek silver coin
showing Alexander
the Great,
4th century B.C.

Moroccan bronze
coins, unseparated
as taken from the
mould, 19th
century

Spanish silver
"piece of eight"
reales from
Mexico,
1732

Gold
10-ducat coin of
Transylvania, 17th century

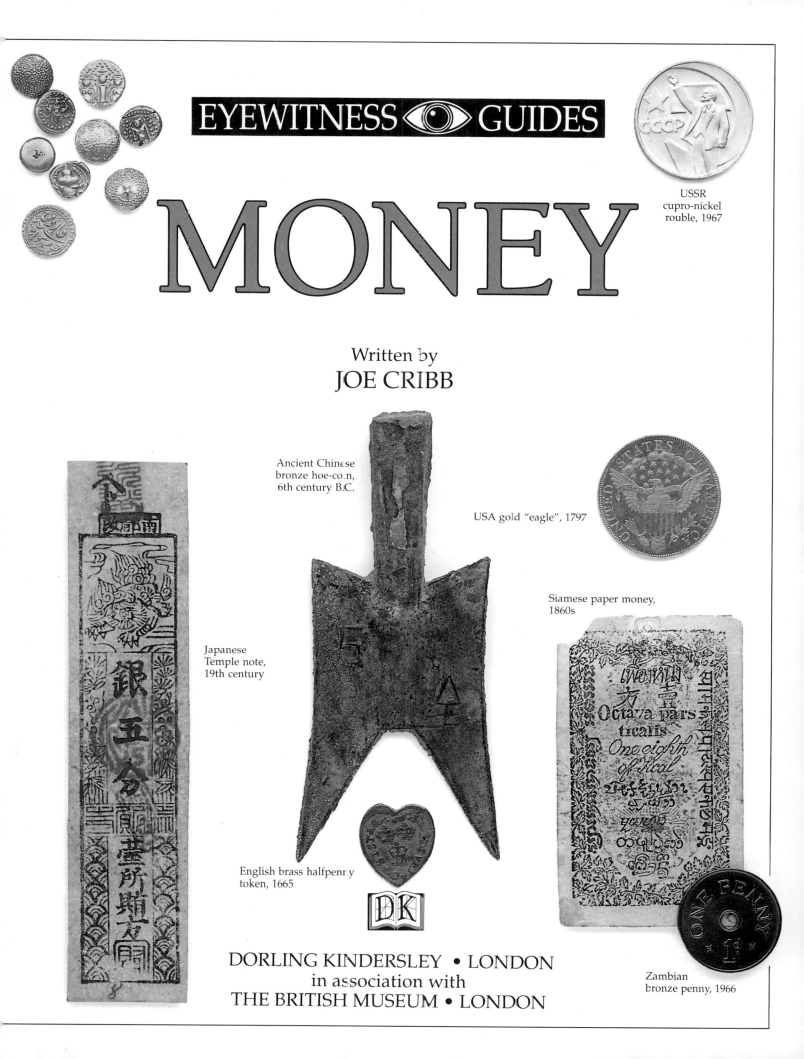

EYEWITNESS ⊙ GUIDES

MONEY

USSR cupro-nickel rouble, 1967

Written by
JOE CRIBB

Ancient Chinese bronze hoe-coin, 6th century B.C.

USA gold "eagle", 1797

Siamese paper money, 1860s

Japanese Temple note, 19th century

English brass halfpenny token, 1665

DK

Zambian bronze penny, 1966

DORLING KINDERSLEY • LONDON
in association with
THE BRITISH MUSEUM • LONDON

English gold sovereign (1901) and brass sovereign balance

Ancient Greek silver: broken coin, cut ingot and wire, from Tarento (Italy) hoard

Ancient Roman silver coin, 3rd century B.C.

Ancient Indian gold coin, 1st century A.D.

Australian aluminium-bronze 2-dollar coin, 1988

Ottoman Turkish gold zeri-mahbub, 18th century

Ancient Roman gold bar made from melted down coins, 4th century

Ancient Chinese bronze knife-coin, 3rd century B.C.

Persian silver wire "larin" coin, 16th century

DK

A DORLING KINDERSLEY BOOK

Project Editor Linda Martin
Art Editor Richard Czapnik
Senior Editor Sophie Mitchell
Senior Art Editor Julia Harris
Editorial Director Sue Unstead
Art Director Anne-Marie Bulat
Special photography Chas Howson, Department of Coins and Medals, The British Museum

This Eyewitness ® Guide has been conceived by Dorling Kindersley Limited and Editions Gallimard

First published in Great Britain in 1990 by Dorling Kindersley Limited, 9 Henrietta Street, London WC2E 8PS

Reprinted 1990, 1991, 1994, 1997

British Library Cataloguing in Publication Data
Cribb, Joe
Money. - (Eyewitness).
1. Money
I. Title   II Series
332.4

ISBN 0 86318-410-3

Colour reproduction by Colourscan, Singapore
Typeset by Windsorgraphics, Ringwood, Hampshire
Printed in Singapore by Toppan Printing Co. (S) Pte Ltd.

Tonga cupro-nickel 1-paanga coin, 1977

Contents

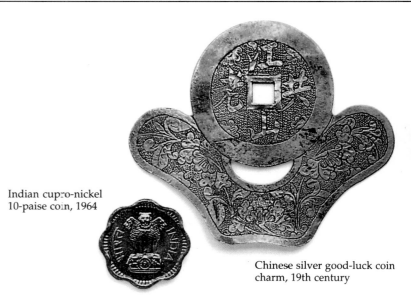

Indian cupro-nickel
10-paise coin, 1964

Chinese silver good-luck coin
charm, 19th century

This is money

IT IS DIFFICULT TO IMAGINE a world without money; every country has its own, and its history reaches back to the earliest written records of human activity. But what is this thing called money? Money can be many different things: for most people it is coins, banknotes, plastic cards, and money in the bank. But for some people in the not too distant past, it has been feathers, stones, beads, and shells (pp. 8-9), for these were the objects they considered valuable. What allows us to describe all these things with the same word, "money", is that they are all an acceptable and recognized means of payment. This even applies to the money you cannot see or feel – the money that is stored in bank computer records, and which can be spent in the same way as the coins and notes in your pocket.

TODAY'S MONEY
Banknotes, coins, and plastic cards come in various shapes, sizes, and colours, but they all share the same name, "money", because they are all used to make payments.

The earliest money

It is not known exactly when money was first used. The oldest written records of it are from Ancient Mesopotamia (now in southern Iraq) about 4,500 years ago. Ancient Mesopotamian cuneiform (wedge-shaped writing) inscriptions describe payments being made with weighed amounts of silver. Since then, weighed amounts of metal have been used as money in many parts of the world, and this practice led to the invention of coins (pp. 10–11).

GOOSE WEIGHT
So that silver and other goods could be weighed accurately, the Ancient Mesopotamians had officially made weights. This example weighs about 30 shekels. There were 60 shekels in a mina.

MESOPOTAMIAN MONEY
The inscription on this tablet commemorates "prices" during the reign of Sin-Kasid of Uruk (B.C. 1865–1804): "In the course of his reign, one shekel [a unit of weight] of silver on the local standard could buy three measures of barley, twelve mina of wool, ten mina of bronze, or three measures of sesame oil, according to the price in his kingdom".

HAMMURABI'S LAWS
This big stone column shows a god giving Hammurabi, King of Babylonia (B.C. 1792–1750) laws referring to how silver should be used. Law 204 says: "If a common man slaps the face of another common man, he must pay ten shekels of silver as compensation".

Ten

Twelve

Wool

Barley

Bronze

CUNEIFORM
The decipherment of cuneiform script has enabled us to discover many other descriptions of money paid in the form of weighed amounts of silver in Ancient Mesopotamia. The characters above appear in the inscription on the tablet.

EGYPTIAN WALL-PAINTING
This Ancient Egyptian wall-painting (14th century B.C.), found in a tomb at Thebes, shows gold rings being weighed on a balance. The Egyptians used balances and weights to measure the value of precious metals.

Lump of gold

STONE WEIGHT
The hieroglyphic inscription on this small Egyptian stone weight is faint, but it tells us that the weight was used for weighing gold. A clearer version of the hieroglyph for "gold" can be seen on an Egyptian gold coin (p. 55).

EGYPTIAN HOARD
The Ancient Egyptians also developed a system for making payments with weighed amounts of metal; records exist of gold, silver, and copper being weighed out as payments. Because the weight set its value, the shape and size of the metal was unimportant. The money was as varied in shape as the bars, rings, and lumps of silver in this 14th-century-B.C. hoard from el-Amarna.

Silver in this form was very convenient as it was easy to cut into smaller bits

Position of string on the scale showed how much the silver in the pan weighed

Ivory rod marked with scale

Heavy silver bar

IN THE BALANCE
Although the Chinese had coins from the 6th century B.C. (p. 11), they did not make gold and silver into coins, but weighed it out for payment – right up to the 1930s. Official weights were made, but for everyday business, traders used small hand-balances like this one. The silver ingots were made in special shapes to show where they came from. The ingots below are all from northeast China, and were made in the 19th century.

Brass counterweight was moved along the scale until the ivory rod hung level

Flower pattern

Burmese weight made of bronze

"FLOWER SILVER"
The only official money in 18th-century Burma was weighed amounts of silver. Most of the silver was poured out into pancake-shaped discs known as "flower silver". The name refers to the patterns on the silver, which were made by blowing through a pipe at the metal as it set.

LION WEIGHT
All the official Burmese weights were in the form of animals such as elephants, ducks, bulls, and lions like this one. A star-shaped mark was stamped on the base of each weight to show that it had been checked by the King's official.

The largest ingot weighs one liang (ounce), and the smallest one weighs one-tenth of one liang. Ingots as heavy as 50 liang were also used

Funny money?

As heavy as stone, as light as a feather, "money" comes in many forms. The objects on these pages may seem very curious, but they were not strange to the people who used them. In some tribal societies, payments were made with objects that had a recognized value: ornaments like shells; tools like hoes; foodstuffs like salt and grain, and cloth (pp. 54–55), all of which were counted out in payments. As with our money today, and the weighed metal money of Ancient Mesopotamia (p. 6), tribal societies had very strict rules about the value and payment of their money; it was generally used to settle social obligations, like marriage payments, compensation, and fines.

MEXICAN MONEY AXE
When the Spanish conquistadors entered Mexico (p. 39), the Mexicans were using cacao (chocolate) beans and small copper axes in payments. The money axes were too fragile to be used as tools!

SUDANESE MONEY HOE
There are many reports from 19th-century Africa of iron hoes being used to make payments in wedding settlements. The Ancient Chinese also made payments with hoes.

STONE MONEY
The stone below is a *small* example of the stone discs used to make social payments and settle disputes by the people of Yap, an island in the Pacific Ocean. The largest examples measured up to 4 m (12 ft) across!

Stone is made of aragonite, a form of limestone

Reed binding to prevent breakage

Herd of African cattle

ETHIOPIAN SALT BAR
Bars of rock salt were widely used both for cooking and as money in Ethiopia until the 1920s. The bars were bound in reeds to prevent breakage. Elsewhere in eastern Africa, herds of cattle are still considered symbols of wealth and status.

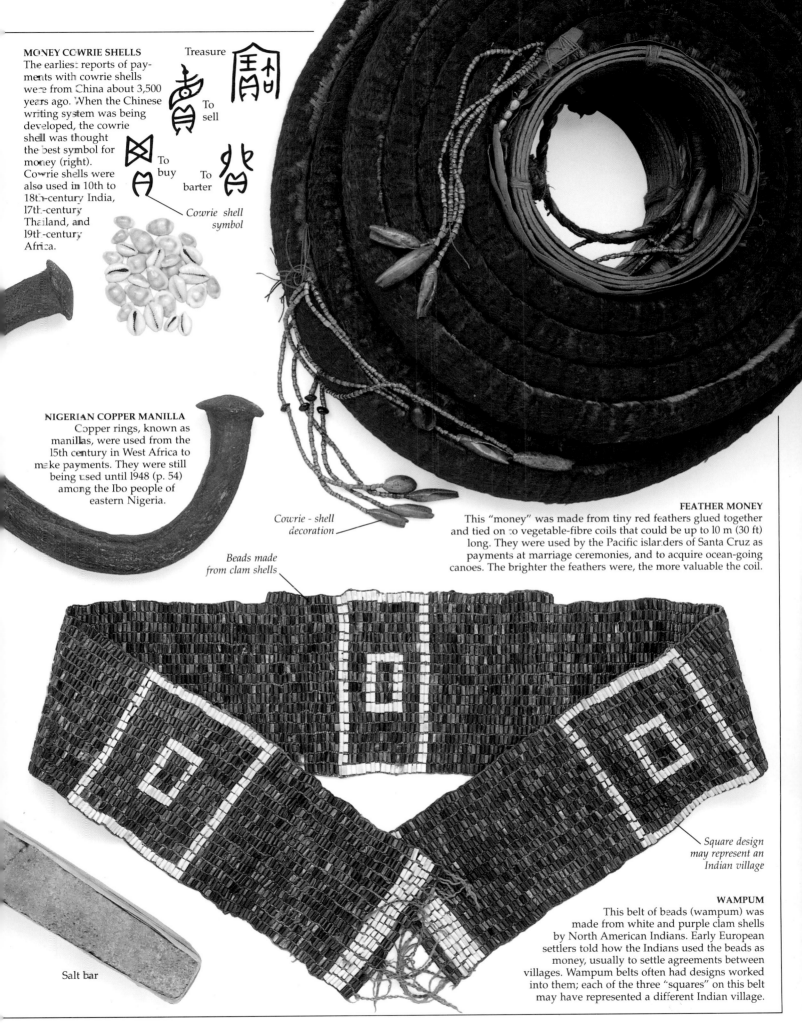

MONEY COWRIE SHELLS

The earliest reports of payments with cowrie shells were from China about 3,500 years ago. When the Chinese writing system was being developed, the cowrie shell was thought the best symbol for money (right). Cowrie shells were also used in 10th to 18th-century India, 17th-century Thailand, and 19th-century Africa.

Treasure

To sell

To buy

To barter

Cowrie shell symbol

NIGERIAN COPPER MANILLA

Copper rings, known as manillas, were used from the 15th century in West Africa to make payments. They were still being used until 1948 (p. 54) among the Ibo people of eastern Nigeria.

Cowrie - shell decoration

Beads made from clam shells

FEATHER MONEY

This "money" was made from tiny red feathers glued together and tied on to vegetable-fibre coils that could be up to 10 m (30 ft) long. They were used by the Pacific islanders of Santa Cruz as payments at marriage ceremonies, and to acquire ocean-going canoes. The brighter the feathers were, the more valuable the coil.

Square design may represent an Indian village

WAMPUM

This belt of beads (wampum) was made from white and purple clam shells by North American Indians. Early European settlers told how the Indians used the beads as money, usually to settle agreements between villages. Wampum belts often had designs worked into them; each of the three "squares" on this belt may have represented a different Indian village.

Salt bar

The first coins

COINS ARE PIECES OF METAL marked with a design that instantly shows that they are money. The earliest-known coins were made during the 7th century B.C. in the kingdom of Lydia (in the country we now call Turkey). Weighed lumps of electrum (a mixture of gold and silver) were used by the Lydians as money, and were stamped with pictures to confirm their weight and therefore their value in payments. This process of stamping is called "minting". The shape of the coins was unimportant. The stamp on the coin was a personal seal or "badge" that identified the person who had guaranteed the coin's weight; the Lydian kings used a lion's head on their coins. This new method of organizing money was a great success and soon spread into Europe. Although the Lydian invention was the first, the same idea was developed elsewhere to standardize other forms of metal money: copper lumps in southern USSR and Italy, bronze tools and shells in China, silver rings in Thailand, and gold and silver bars in Japan.

Mark made by punches

One-stater coins

LYDIAN ELECTRUM COINS
The weight of Lydian money was measured in units called "staters", about 14 g (1/2 oz) each. Fractional coins were also made; coins as small as 1/96 stater were made! Each metal lump was placed on an anvil, and the punches were pushed into the lump with a hammer. Because the anvil had been engraved with the lion's head emblem of the Lydian kings, these coins (B.C. 600) now had this image stamped on them.

1/6-stater coins

1/24-stater coin

Greek letters

Marked ingot made of copper

PERSONAL SEALS
The Greek letters on the coin from western Turkey (left) mean "I am the seal of Phanes". The design is similar to the Greek seal (above) which names its owner, Mandronax.

Caria, c. B.C. 530

Andros, c. B.C. 525

Ceos, c. B.C. 525

Aegina, c. B.C. 540

Athens, c. B.C. 540

EARLY SILVER COINS
The idea of coinage spread from western Turkey into the Greek world. Within 100 years, coins were issued as far away as Italy and Libya. The pictures on four of these coins were the emblems of the place of issue: a lion for Caria in Turkey; a vase, a squid, and a turtle for the Aegean islands of Andros, Ceos, and Aegina. The beetle is the emblem of an Athenian official. These coins can be dated because they were buried as an offering to the goddess Artemis (right) in the foundations of her temple at Ephesus, built around B.C. 560.

Knife-shaped coin

Hoe-shaped coin

Olbian dolphin coins,
4th century B.C.

Olbian round coin,
4th century B.C.

CAST COPPER COINS

Before coinage was adopted in Olbia in the USSR, and in Rome and other Latin and Etruscan (pre-Roman) cities of central Italy, weighed pieces of cast copper were used as money. Under the influence of Greek coins, designs were added to these copper ingots (pieces of cast metal made in a mould) to turn them into coins. In Olbia, most of the cast copper pieces were round, but some were cast in the shape of a dolphin, probably because Olbia was on the Black Sea coast.

Cowrie-shell-shaped coin

CHINESE TOOL AND SHELL COINS

The earliest Chinese coins (about B.C. 500) were made from bronze in the shape of the tools and cowrie shells that had previously been used as money by the Chinese. The tool-shaped coins were too fragile to be used as actual tools!

ELEPHANT-SIZED COIN!

In Rome, the earliest marked ingots kept the rectangular shape used earlier for unmarked ingots. The Indian elephant shown here is a reference to the war elephants of a Greek army that invaded southern Italy in B.C. 280.

JAPANESE SHOGUN

Shoguns were fearsome military dictators who ruled Japan from the 12th to the 19th century.

THAI RING-COINS

Before they made coins, the people of Thailand used weighed silver rings as money. When the rings were made into coins (17th century), their shape was changed by bending or hammering. They were then stamped with official marks.

Gold coin, 1601

JAPANESE INGOT COINS

During the late 16th and early 17th centuries, the Japanese leader Ieyasu, who later became the first Tokugawa Shogun, reorganized Japan's monetary system (p. 52). His gold and silver coins were in the form of hammered or cast slabs, like the ingots previously used as money.

Silver coin, 1601

Gold coin, 1818

The first paper money

BANKNOTES ARE ONLY PIECES OF PAPER, yet they are accepted as money because it is what they *represent* that is valuable. It was the Chinese who first saw the advantages of handling money in the form of printed paper documents. During the 10th century, the Chinese government issued heavy iron coins that were worth little. People started to leave their coins with merchants and to use the handwritten receipts the merchants gave them instead. In the early 11th century, the government took over from the merchants and printed receipts that could be used officially as money, and to make the system simpler, the receipts were given fixed values.

DIFFICULT TO LOSE!
The banknote below was quite large to carry around. The largest note ever issued, it measured 22.8 x 33 cm (9 x 13 in).

JAPANESE NOTE
The idea of paper money spread to Japan during the 17th century. Most Japanese notes were issued by feudal clans and temples.

Japanese "bookmark" note of 1746

TEMPLE MONEY
Japanese temples – like this one in Kyoto – acted like banks, issuing their own paper money.

CHINESE PAPER MONEY
In the centre of the design of this 14th-century Chinese note, you can just see the 1,000 coins it represented. The coins would have weighed about 3.5 kg (8 lb). Perhaps it is not surprising that the Chinese were the first to use paper money!

ENGLISH MONEY ORDER
Before official printed banknotes appeared in Europe, handwritten paper "money" had long been in use. This note (1665) was addressed by a John Lewis to the London money lenders, Morriss and Clayton, asking them to pay 50 pounds of his money to his servant.

SWEDISH BANKNOTE

In 1661, during a time of shortage of silver coins, the Swedish Stockholm Bank began to issue Europe's first printed paper money. This note (1666) represented 100 dalers (pp. 44–45).

Wax seal

JOHN LAW

The Scotsman, John Law, was responsible for the issue of paper money in France.

NORWEGIAN MERCHANT'S NOTE

Following the Swedish example, a Norwegian merchant, Jorgen Thor Mohlen, issued printed notes for circulation as money (1695). Mohlen used the coins exchanged to fund his business.

BANK OF SCOTLAND NOTE

During the late 17th century, printed paper money began to be issued in Britain. The Bank of Scotland issued notes valued in Scottish money, like this one dated 1723. Twelve Scottish pounds were equal to one English pound.

FRENCH ROYAL BANKNOTE

It was a Scotsman, John Law, who introduced the idea of printed paper money to France. In 1718, the bank that he had set up in Paris received the French king's approval to issue notes valued in silver coin. However, the bank issued too many notes, and they became worthless.

ITALIAN PAPAL NOTE

This 31-scudi note of the Bank of the Holy Spirit at Rome was issued in 1786, during the reign of Pope Pius VI, for circulation in the Papal States. The bank, established by Pope Paul V in 1605, was Europe's first national bank.

NEW JERSEY "BILL"

When the British government failed to supply its North American colonies with coins, the colonies decided to issue their own paper money called bills (p. 28).

COMMERCIAL BANKNOTE

Commercial banks have played a large part in the growth of the role of paper money. This note was issued in 1954 in Hong Kong by the Chartered Bank, a London-based commercial bank with branches in every continent.

How coins are made

An artist prepares the designs

A COIN IS MADE by marking a blank piece of metal with designs – a process called "minting". The designs are stamped on to the metal by pressing it between two hard metal surfaces called dies. This is the basic method invented 2,600 years ago to make the first coins; the dies were an anvil and punch, and the designs were engraved on the anvil by hand (p. 10). Today the dies are part of a huge, electrically powered machine press.

Electrically powered machines are also used to make the "blanks" (unmarked coin-shaped pieces of metal) and to imprint the designs on to the dies. Today's coinmaking techniques are shown here through the production of the 1973 European Economic Community coin at the British Royal Mint in Llantrisant, Wales.

1973
50
PENCE

PLASTER MODEL
Once the designs for the coin are approved, an artist makes a large plaster model from them. The fine details of the design are cut into the plaster with metal tools. The more detailed the designs are, the more difficult it is for anybody to forge the coin.

ELECTROTYPE
After the plaster model has been made, a metal version (below) is produced by a complex process called "electrotyping".

Electrotype has a hard nickel face with copper backing

REDUCING MACHINE
A rod on this machine connects a metal point to a drill. The point traces the contours of the electrotype's surface and the drill cuts a much smaller version on to a steel punch (below left).

The reducing machine cuts this reduction punch

The punch (left) stamps the design on this tool, a matrix

Part of a copper bar, called a "pig", of the type used at the Mint

ROLLING MILL
Once the cupro-nickel alloy has been cast into slabs, it is rolled several times until it is thin enough to use.

CUPRO-NICKEL
The 1973 European Economic Community coin was made from an alloy called cupro-nickel. Pure copper and nickel are combined to make this alloy. Copper is a cheap metal but is very soft, so a small proportion of nickel is added to harden it. This alloy is also appropriate for making higher-denomination coins because they used to be made of silver, and cupro-nickel is a silver-coloured alloy.

Raw nickel reaches the Mint in the form of pellets

Blanks are softened in a special furnace. This process is called "annealing"

A slab of cupro-nickel alloy after the first rolling

Softened blanks are cleaned in acid. This process is called "pickling"

Coin-shaped blanks are cut out by a blanking press

Metal strip with holes is called "scissel"

MAKING BLANKS
Once the cupro-nickel strip is the correct thickness, it is passed through a press that stamps the blanks out of it. The remaining strip, full of holes, is called "scissel". The scissel is melted down to make more strips. The blanks are softened and cleaned, ready for the final act of striking in the coining press.

THE END RESULT
This British 50-pence coin (actual size) was issued in 1973 to commemorate British entry into the European Economic Community. Its strange shape makes it difficult for forgers to copy.

The end result

The matrix (left) stamps this working punch

The working punch (left) is used to make this die

COINING PRESS
The blanks are finally delivered to the coining press, into which the die (left) has been fitted, together with the die for the front of the coin. The blank is then squashed between these dies. It is difficult for anybody to forge coins without having access to this sophisticated machinery.

Thin strip cut from roll

How banknotes are made

MAKING BANKNOTES is a secret and complicated business, because banknote printers have to make sure that notes are as difficult as possible for forgers to copy (pp. 18–19). Some of the less confidential aspects are revealed here through the work of one of the world's most successful banknote printers; you can see how they produce a specimen note to show to their customers. Four main stages are involved: design, papermaking, ink-mixing, and printing. The printing is done by three separate processes: lithography, intaglio, and letterpress. The materials created for each of these stages and processes are different for every banknote design used.

Two sharp engraving tools called burins are used for cutting the design into the plate

A burnisher is used for smoothing the flat surface

MAGNIFYING GLASS
The engraver needs a magnifying glass to work on the tiny details of the design that make it hard for a forger to copy the note.

SECURITY THREAD
Once made of metal, this plastic thread is enclosed in the paper as it is made. This feature is one of the most difficult for forgers to copy accurately.

INTAGLIO PRINTING PLATE
The main features of the design are printed from a steel intaglio plate. The features are hand-engraved, back-to-front, into a plate with sharp tools. Only the engraved area on the plate is inked, leaving the flat surface clean.

INTAGLIO PROOF
This is a sample printing from the intaglio plate. Intense pressure during printing causes the ink to be drawn out of the engraved areas and to stand slightly raised on the paper, so that it can be felt with your fingers. Some banks use this form of printing to add identification marks for the blind (p. 35).

FIRST SKETCHES

An artist draws sketches for the proposed note. The sketch (left) shows the position of the main features, and the sketch below, details of the coloured background. When the designs are approved, preparation for printing begins.

Blue sheet

Yellow sheet

Red sheet

LITHOGRAPHY PROOFS

The background design is printed by a system called offset lithography. The different coloured inks (eight for this note) are separated into three groups: blues, reds, and yellows. One printing plate is photographically made for each group. The ink on each plate is transferred on to a single rubber-covered cylinder that prints the combined image. The trial sheets above show the image from each plate separately, and the combined images as they appear on the printed note.

Sheet showing combined images

PAPERMAKING

Banknotes have to be tough, so they are printed on special paper made from cotton fibres. Often a watermark and security thread are included to deter forgery. This picture shows Portals Paper Mill, England, as it was in 1854.

NUMBERING MACHINE

The final printing process is the traditional letterpress method, using a numbering machine to print a different serial number on each note. The numbers cannot be included in the intaglio or lithography plates because they change for each note. Signatures, which also change regularly, may be printed by this method.

INKS

These eight inks have been mixed from 22 colours to give the exact combination of colours needed for this note. They include invisible, secret, security features as yet another measure to make forgery difficult, and are only used for printing banknotes and other documents of value.

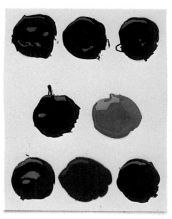

THE END RESULT

Specimens like this note will be used by Thomas de la Rue to show their customers the latest security features developed to protect notes from being forged. They will be shown to banks in countries as far apart as New Zealand, Nepal, Botswana, and Peru, as well as to banks in the United Kingdom, the Channel Islands, and Europe.

THOMAS DE LA RUE
AND COMPANY LIMITED
1422 WILLIAM CAXTON 1491
PROOF NO. 398 2/5

Forgery and fakes

Imprisonment is the most common form of punishment for forgers caught in the act today, although heavy fines are also used to deter would-be criminals

FORGERY, THE ART OF MAKING FALSE MONEY, has always been considered a very serious crime. In the past, punishments for forgery included deportation, having your hands cut off, being boiled alive, and execution! However, driven on by the profit to be made by turning inexpensive pieces of metal or paper into something of value, forgers continue to break the law, although these days the punishment is more likely to be a large fine or imprisonment. Not only do forgers harm the individuals taken in by their deceit, they also cheat the state by whose authority money is issued. Despite all the devices adopted by coinmakers (pp. 14–15) and banknote printers (pp. 16–17) to make forgeries impossible, there are still plenty of forgers prepared to overcome these difficulties, take the risks, and, if caught, face the consequences!

PLATED FORGERIES
Instead of solid gold, these copies of Greek coins were made from gold-plated copper. They were recognized as forgeries when the plating cracked to reveal the green copper underneath.

Silver case

Tin disc

TIN DOLLAR
This Chinese forgery of a Mexican silver dollar, found in Shanghai in the 1930s, was made by enclosing a tin disc in a thin silver case.

Round half-crown coin cut to the shape of a 50-pence piece

Genuine coin

Lead cast

COPIES
The two copies of a British 50-pence were meant to deceive those not familiar with the new coin. One is made from lead, the other is cut from an old, round coin.

Non-existent bank

NON-EXISTENT BANK
When Italy was short of small change during the 1970s (p. 37), some Italian banks made small-change notes. An enterprising forger printed his own notes, but in the name of a bank that did not exist!

HANDRAWN FORGERY
All the details on this false Swedish 10-daler banknote of 1868 were copied by hand. This was undoubtedly a time-consuming, but presumably, profitable task for the forger!

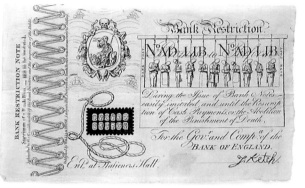

THE HANGMAN'S NOOSE
This cartoon (reduced) is in the form of a Bank of England
note. It criticizes the severe punishment for using forged notes,
and shows Britannia (the Bank's emblem) eating children,
and the pound sign as a hangman's noose.

Checking change

In order to protect themselves from the loss suffered by receiving a
forged coin or note, traders have always been very careful to check all
the money paid to them. When money was in the form of gold and
silver coins, the best precaution was to check that the quality of gold
or silver was up to scratch, and that each
coin contained the full weight of
precious metal. There
were various
ways of
doing
this.

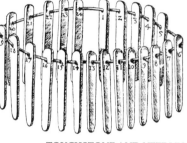

TOUCHSTONE AND NEEDLES
To check the quality of a gold coin,
a trader would mark the black
touchstone with the equivalent gold
carat touch needle (above), and then
compare that mark with the mark
the coin left. The streaks here (left to
right) were made with 24, 9, 12, 15, 18, and
22-carat gold.

24-carat gold coin

Greek silver coin,
5th century

*Punch to
test coin
was not
plated*

Portuguese
Indian coin,
1688

CHECKED COINS
In order to be sure
that a coin was not
plated, traders would cut
into the surface, as with the Greek coin. The
Indian coin has been checked with small
engraved punches.

DIRECTIONS for using Mr S. HENRY'S
Royal Patent Ballance & Gauge for Gold Coin of the last & present Reign,
(Agreeable to the last Regulation.)

1ly Put your Coin in the swinging Pan and to
weigh a Guinea slide the weight home to
the end of the Beam, for a Half Guinea advance it forward home to the small Pin,
then press the Brass Lever in the middle &
the weight will be determined: the Quarter
Guinea is weighed the same as the Half—

Guinea by putting the Quarter Guinea weight
in the Pan with the Quarter Guinea.— 2ly
Apply your Coin to the Gauge, the large stroke
for the Guinea, the middle one for the Half and
the small one for the Quarter &c. if they Pass
through (on turning them all round) be assured
they are not Counterfeits. pr 18. 6d

Sold in London Wholesale by James Stamp, Goldsmith, Cheapside, Woolley, and Heming,
Hardwaremen, Cheapside, Stibbs, and Deane, Hardwaremen, Fish Street Hill.

COIN BALANCE AND WEIGHTS
This British cased-balance was used
in the 18th century to weigh gold coins.
The brass weights above are from 17th-century Belgium,
and are varied so that foreign gold coins imported into the
area from the Netherlands, France, England, Scotland, Italy,
Portugal, Hungary, and Morocco could be weighed.

*A plated coin of the right weight would
be too thick to go through this slot*

Money and trade

MONEY IS at the centre of trade, whether it takes place in the village shop or on the international commodities (products) market. Money, the "medium of exchange", enables both buyer and seller to agree to part with what they have in order to get what they want. In the days when money took the form of precious metals such as gold and silver, heavy chests of coins were shipped around the world in trade! However, sometimes the money itself stayed still, but the ownership of it was transferred by pieces of paper called bills of exchange. Today, money rarely moves in trade. Although bills of exchange are still in use, most international payments are made by telephone and computer (pp. 58–59).

DUTCH TRADERS' MANUAL
During the 16th century, so many foreign coins were handled by Dutch merchants that they used handbooks to identify current coins from other lands and to indicate their value. The one here was published in Antwerp in 1580. These pages show Scandinavian silver dalers (pp. 42–45).

OWLS EVERYWHERE!
The silver coins of Athens (right) were known as "owls" because of their design; the Little Owl was the special bird of the goddess Athena. Athens was the richest city of Ancient Greece, and traded throughout the world with its silver coins. The design was so popular that many countries issued coins with a similar design, as you can see from this map.

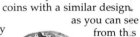

Turkey

Italy

Athens

Palestine

Iraq

Iran

Egypt

Southern Arabia

Daelder van Denemercke.

Daelder van Sweden.

Daelder van Sweden.

Daelder van Sweden.

Daelder van Denemercke.

Daelder van Sweden.

BARTER
International trade today is often carried out without money; tractors are swapped for jam, and grain for oil. This form of trade, known as "barter", has a long history; the earliest record of it comes from Ancient Egypt, 4,500 years ago. The main problem with barter is deciding how many pots of jam each tractor is worth!

Canada

Australia

Great Britain

PIECES OF EIGHT
Spanish "pieces of eight' (8-reales coins) were popularly known as "dollars". The Spanish empire exported so many of these in trade that they were adopted in many countries as official money, but were stamped or cut for local use. The coins here all came from the Spanish mint in Mexico City. In China, the dollar became the standard form of money until the 1930s (p. 52).

British West Africa

West Indies

China

DOLLAR NOTE
After the end of Spanish rule in the Americas, the new republics, including Mexico, continued to issue dollars for export to China. This Mexican dollar note was printed for a British trade bank to issue in China.

Chinese gold bar salvaged from the wreck of a merchant ship

CHINESE GOLD
Spanish silver "pieces of eight" were traded with China in exchange for gold. Gold bars like this were shipped back to Europe where they were made into coins. This bar was found in the wreck of a merchant ship sailing from China to Europe.

BILL OF EXCHANGE
Coins are no longer used in international trade, and money is usually paid by telephone messages between bank computers or by written instructions like this bill of exchange. A bill of exchange is a written order signed by one trader, instructing a second person, or bank, to pay from his account a specified amount in a specified currency to the other trader by a specified date.

Money in war

ALEXANDER THE GREAT
This silver coin (slightly enlarged) was made by Alexander the Great in B.C. 326 to commemorate his defeat of an Indian king. The king is on an elephant.

SIEGE GOLD
During the siege of Athens by the Spartans in B.C. 406, silver owl coins (p. 20) ran out. The Athenians had to melt down golden statues of the goddess of victory to make these coins!

THROUGHOUT HISTORY, money and war seem to have marched along hand in hand. Money plays a large part in the preparations for war as it buys the necessary arms and encourages men to become soldiers. Mercenary soldiers are offered huge sums of money to fight for a foreign country. The hardships of war led to the issue of new forms of money in cities under siege (cut off and surrounded by the enemy) and by governments that ran out of money. The same circumstances have also brought into circulation unofficial forms of money such as cigarettes. Too often money provides the reward for success in war; in the past, soldiers have frequently been recruited on the understanding that they would be paid from the booty captured from the enemy.

SIEGE NOTE
When a Prussian army besieged French revolutionary forces in the German city of Mainz in 1793, the French army issued "emergency" notes for use within the city. These notes were of French denomination.

CHARLES I OF ENGLAND
Charles I issued this coin in 1644 at his Oxford mint after his opponents in Parliament (Roundheads) took over his London mint.

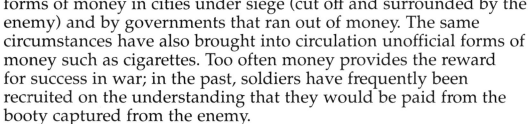

No. 9506 *Monnoye de Siège Trois Livres à échanger contre du numéraire.*

3 Livres.

SIEGE DE MAYENCE MAI 1793 2E DE LA REP. FRANC:

During the English Civil War (1642–1648), Cavaliers fought the Roundheads for control of the country

SIEGE SILVER
In 1644, Royalist troops (Cavaliers), besieged in Scarborough Castle in northern England, cut up silver plates to make coins. The castle and denomination were stamped on each coin.

CONFEDERATE NOTES
In 1864, during the American Civil War, the southern Confederate States financed the war by issuing notes for repayment in coin two years after the war had ended.

Confederate forces, flag flying, storm a Yankee-held fort during the American Civil War

Distortion caused by blow of bullet

BOER WAR BADGES
These patriotic badges show the British Commander-in-Chief, Lord Roberts (top), and one of his officers, Colonel Baden-Powell (below), who issued the Mafeking siege notes. Baden-Powell later founded the Scouting Movement.

LIFE SAVERS!
During Europe's Thirty Years War, many German soldiers carried a St. George thaler (top left) because they believed it would stop bullets. At the Battle of Culloden, Scotland, an English soldier was saved from death by the copper halfpenny (right), which bears the mark of the bullet it deflected.

Boer coins

BOER WAR MONEY
Emergency issues of money were made by both the Boers and the British during this war in South Africa. In 1900, the British, who were besieged by the Boers at Mafeking, issued notes like the one above. After the loss of Pretoria and their mint, the Boers retreated and issued gold pound coins from a blacksmith's shop.

Mount inscribed "Nov 9 1914 HMAS SYDNEY and SMS EMDEN"

WAR BOOTY
This Mexican silver dollar, mounted to be worn as a medal, was part of the booty captured from a German ship by an Australian crew in 1914.

"FROM FRED TO NELLIE"
A British soldier made this coin into a keepsake for his wife when he left to fight in France during the First World War.

DESERT RAT MONEY
Allied troops serving in Libya, North Africa, during the Second World War were paid in Italian lire notes, the currency of this former Italian colony.

REVOLUTIONARY NOTE
A large issue of notes, like the one above for 10 pesos, was made in 1900 by the provincial treasury at Ocana in Colombia, South America, to pay soldiers serving in the revolutionary army of General Urribe.

SMOKE OR SPEND?
At the end of the Second World War, a shortage of coins and notes in Europe meant that other desirable objects came into use as money. Cigarettes, food, and clothing, all in short supply, became an acceptable means of payment. Unfortunately, there was no Hammurabi's column (p. 6) to fix a scale of payments!

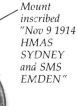

GREEK OCCUPATION MONEY
Italian lire were also used in Greece by the occupying Italian army. This note was issued in 1944 for use in Rhodes. As well as the Roman twins, Romulus and Remus, and the wolf that suckled them, there are pictures of two coins from ancient Rhodes.

The power of money

IT HAS BEEN SAID that the love of money is the root of all evil, and it certainly seems to be for some people; misers love their own money and thieves love other people's! Money has led many people into crime but, curiously, money also has the reputation of bringing luck. Who can deny the obvious increase in good fortune of those who have a lot of it! There are many curious beliefs about the power of money for good. Since ancient times, coins have been used to drive off demons, to ensure a safe journey after death, to cure the plague, to protect in battle, and to promise everlasting love.

The Phoenician god, Melqart, appears on the front of these silver shekels

KING MIDAS
Perhaps the most famous story of greed is the legend of King Midas, who asked the gods to give him the ability to turn all he touched into gold. It was not a kind gift, as he soon discovered. His pleasure soon turned to pain as food, drink, and, finally, his favourite daughter also turned to gold!

The root of all evil

Murder, robbery, arson, and bribery – where there is crime, there is money. Money itself is surely not evil, it is nothing more than a necessary part of everyday life. So why does it so often appear as the motive for crime? Are greed and envy, or poverty and need the causes, or is it because criminals see in money the means of achieving the good fortune they seem to lack?

COIN CLIPPINGS
Before the invention of coinmaking machines, coins were not perfectly round. It was easy to trim a bit off the edge of silver coins for melting down without anyone noticing so that the coins could still be spent. These coils were clipped from silver English coins in the late 17th century. During William III's reign (1689-1702), people were executed in London for this crime.

BEWARE. . . PIRATES!
Spanish treasure fleets shipping silver "pieces of eight" and gold doubloons from Mexico to Europe (pp. 38–39) were the main target of pirates. As they had few opportunities to spend their loot, pirates often buried their treasure, saving it for their "retirement fund"!

These coins were issued by the Chinese emperor Kangxi, and the characters of his name, meaning health and prosperity, appear on the coins

Keepsake for a child who died aged 18 months

MARY RAMSHAW BORN MAY Yᵉ 4 1773 AGED 18 MONTH DIED OCTᵣ 10 1774

Hearts and doves symbolizing love

JEATT DARTMOUTH

LOVE TOKENS AND KEEPSAKES
In Britain and America, it used to be the custom for engaged couples to exchange coins as pledges of their love (top). Tokens were also made as keepsakes of dead loved ones (centre), a transported convict (bottom), or to commemorate a birth (right).

Willm Culling BORN April 30ᵗʰ 1790

THIRTY PIECES OF SILVER

One of the world's most famous crimes, the betrayal of Jesus by one of his followers, Judas, had its cash reward: 30 pieces of silver. The coins in question are thought to have been silver shekels from the Phoenician city of Tyre. Tyrian shekels were the only silver coins available in quantity in 1st-century Palestine.

ARE YOU A MISER?

Looking after your money is no bad thing (p. 56), but if you become so mean that you will not spend any of it either on yourself or others, then you have undoubtedly become a victim of the power of money!

Demon-dispelling sword for driving off a fever demon

Red is a lucky colour for the Chinese

Corpse hands over his fare to Charon the ferryman

HEALING SWORD AND COINS

This demon-dispelling Chinese coin sword was made to hang above the bed of sick people to ward off evil spirits. Instead of a sword, a coin-shaped exorcism charm (top right) could be used. In Britain, monarchs gave sick subjects a gold coin (centre) to help cure them. In Germany, silver medals like the one to the right were thought to protect you from the plague.

Money myth and magic

It is not difficult to see why money is seen as a source of good fortune. Until we look closely, rich people always seem to be blessed with all the good fortune they need. They can afford to buy all the material goods they need to make their life happy. However, there is a more magical, spiritual side to money. The pictures and words on coins often add to their "power" to bring good luck.

"ANY FARES PLEASE"?

According to mythology, the Ancient Greeks put a silver coin, "obol", into the mouth of a corpse to pay Charon, the ferryman, to take the corpse across the River Styx into Hades. The coin (left) was found in the mouth of a Persian corpse.

This note claims to be an issue of the Bank of Hell

HOLY COINS

Travellers wore the silver coin charm (top left) to gain the protection of St. George, patron saint of horsemen. Indian Muslims carried the name of Mohammed on the copy of a square silver rupee (top right). The image of the monkey god, Hanuman, on the round silver rupee (right) gave comfort to Hindus.

HELL MONEY

The Chinese send money to their dead ancestors by regularly burning special banknotes like the one here.

The monkey god, Hanuman, guardian of those in need

One million dollars!

A STICKY BUSINESS
A Penny Black stamp like the one above could cost anything between £140 and £2,750, depending on its condition. However, a Penny Blue is even more costly; you could expect to pay between £300 and £5,500 for one of those.

Iᴏ ʏᴏᴜ ᴡᴇʀᴇ suddenly to become a millionaire, what would you do with your fabulous wealth? Would you rush out and spend it all straight away, would you plan carefully what you were going to do with it all – perhaps investing and saving some of it for the future – or would you save it all, never spending or giving any of it away? If you were to rush out to the shops in order to spend it, you might well find that is more difficult than you imagined! Like most young millionaires, you would probably spend quite a lot of it on designer-clothes, records, tapes, computers, hi-fis and holidays, but you would still have a considerable amount left. You may start collecting something, like rare stamps, old books, antique dolls or old coins.

Roman coin of the Emperor Diocletian, (A.D. 284–305)

Queen Anne coin (1703) made from captured Spanish treasure

Ancient Greek coin, (c. B.C. 460)

RARE COINS
These three coins (actual size) are all worth thousands of pounds each. The Roman gold coin (top left), the English gold five-guinea coin of Queen Anne (top right), and the Ancient Greek silver 10-drachma coin (bottom) are not valuable because they are beautiful, but simply because they are rare. However, you do not need to be a millionaire to collect coins (pp. 60–61).

STACKS OF MONEY
There are 10,000 one-hundred dollar bills in this pile – a total of one million dollars.
It is thought that the richest man in the world is the Sultan of Brunei, whose fortune is estimated at around 25,000 million US dollars.

Modern
gambling chips

GOING, GOING, GONE!

Auction rooms are where people can spend a lot of money – often much more than they intended to. The bid for the painting in this picture has reached £60,000 – $US97,260, almost one-tenth of the stack of dollars on this page.

MONTE CARLO MADNESS

Some people enjoy gambling with their money. For them, the excitement of playing games of chance to increase their fortune is an addiction. Even if they lose, they still dream of winning a fortune. Monte Carlo, a town in Monaco on the Riviera in southeast France, is perhaps the most famous gambling centre for the rich. This gambling chip is for one million francs, and would have been used in the 1930s.

The roll of dice can win or lose a fortune

If you are clever, or lucky, at cards, your fortune may increase. If you are not clever, or unlucky, it may disappear altogether!

FINE WINE?

Buying old wine is a gamble not many people put to the test. The wine of Chateau Lafite is renowned, and a bottle of 1902 vintage like this would cost around £350 at auction. However, there is a high risk that wine of such an age will be totally undrinkable, so most collectors prefer to leave the bottle unopened; it would seem that they derive sufficient satisfaction from just looking at the bottle to justify such an outlay!

The United States of America

T HE CURRENCY OF THE UNITED STATES of America is made up of dollars and cents. Coins and paper money were first introduced into North America by various European settlers. But Britain did not issue coins or notes for its settlers, so they used tobacco, shell beads (pp. 8–9), and imported Spanish coins, "pieces of eight"(known as "dollars"), instead. The colonists (settlers) also issued their own paper money called "bills". The dollar had already been chosen as the currency of the United States of America before the Declaration of Independence was signed on 4th July l776. The first US dollars were paper – the Continental Currency bills issued from 1775; silver dollars were also issued from 1794. The US dollar, made of paper again since 1862, is the world's most widely used currency.

The American bald eagle

BRITISH COLONIAL MONEY
The British colonists did not have any British coins. Instead they used beads and tobacco, and made their own coins and paper money. This was denominated in pounds, shillings, and pence, like these Massachusetts shillings of 1652 and Pennsylvanian four-pence note of 1755.

FIRST COINS OF THE UNITED STATES
After a period of planning and experiment, the United States began in 1793 to issue a regular coinage based on the dollar. The 1793 copper cent (top right) was followed by the silver dollar in 1794 (top centre), and the gold 10-dollar "eagle" in 1795 (top left). The size of the cent was based on the British halfpenny, and the dollar on the Spanish "piece of eight".

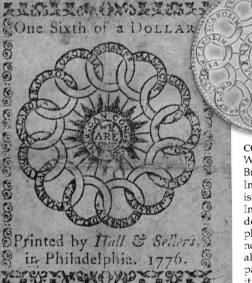

Chain on this tin pattern represents the 13 states united against Britain

CONTINENTAL CURRENCY
When the colonists broke with Britain, they financed their War of Independence with paper dollars issued by the Continental Congress. In 1776 a silver dollar was planned, but not introduced, although tin patterns for it exist.

LEAF MONEY
Tobacco leaves were made into bundles and officially used as money in Virginia and Maryland in the 17th and 18th centuries.

ENTER WHO DARES!
Fort Knox in Kentucky has been the site of the United States Gold Bullion Depository since 1938. The gold is stored in concrete and steel vaults inside a bomb-proof building that is protected by guards armed with machine guns.

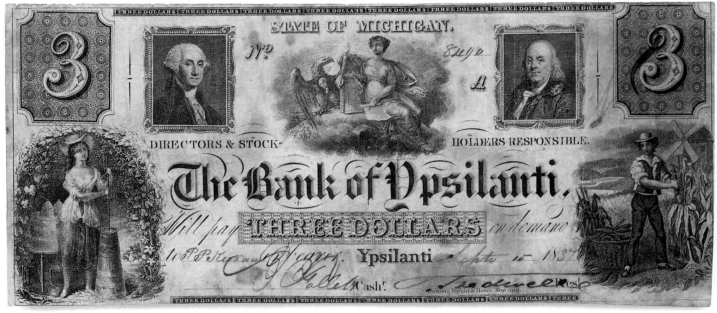

THREE-DOLLAR BILL

During the 19th century, most of the money used in the United States was in the form of paper dollars. This note was issued in 1837 by a small private bank in Ypsilanti, Michigan.

GOLD RUSH!

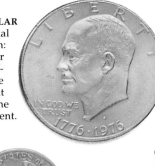

After the discovery of gold in California in 1848, gold dust and nuggets were used as money in the mining camps. When the gold reached San Francisco, the centre of the gold-mining area, it was made into coins like this 50-dollar piece made in 1852.

EISENHOWER DOLLAR

Recent coins have a presidential portrait as their main design: Eisenhower on the dollar (right); Kennedy on the half-dollar; Washington on the quarter; Franklin D. Roosevelt on the dime; Jefferson on the nickel; and Lincoln on the cent.

BICENTENNIAL QUARTER

In 1976, as part of the celebrations of the 200th anniversary of American Independence, commemorative coins like this one were issued.

FAILED DOLLAR

In 1979, a dollar coin portraying the feminist leader, Susan B. Anthony, was issued. It was not popular, and was withdrawn from use. There are now 441 million Susan B. Anthony dollars under lock and key, awaiting their fate!

DEPRESSION FOOD QUEUE

After the Great Crash of 1929, the value of the dollar fell drastically. By the end of 1931, 4,000 banks had closed. There was massive unemployment, and many people had to rely on charity to eat, queuing up for regular food handouts.

Today's money

LAS VEGAS

Dollar coins still survive in the casinos of Las Vegas and Atlantic City, New Jersey, where they are poured into the slots of "one-arm bandit" gambling machines.

In the USA, the coins above are called a "quarter", "dime", "nickel", and "penny" respectively

See pages 62–63

France

TODAY, FRANCE'S MONEY consists of francs divided into centimes. The oldest-known French money is Greek silver coins made in Massilia (Marseilles) almost 2,500 years ago. From the second century B.C., the Gauls (Celtic peoples of ancient France) issued coins that copied Greek designs, but when the Romans conquered the Gauls, they brought their own coins with them. Roman coin designs remained in use until the Frankish kings began to issue silver deniers, the first truly French coins. The franc, first issued as a gold coin in 1360, and as a silver coin in 1577, did not become the main unit of French currency until 1795. It has retained this position ever since, but its value has changed many times as the result of revolutions and war. The last major change was in 1960 when a new franc was issued worth 100 of the francs in use until then.

The Greek goddess Artemis (p. 10)

PATRON SAINT OF COINMAKERS
St. Eligius, the patron saint of coinmakers and goldsmiths, worked at the Paris mint during the 7th century for the Merovingian kings of Gaul. In this stained-glass panel he is shown using traditional tools for making coins (p. 10).

CELTIC GOLD
The head of the Greek god Apollo on this gold coin (B.C. 100) was copied by the Celts from an earlier Greek coin.

GREEK SILVER COINS
During the 5th century B.C., the Greek colony at Massilia issued small silver coins with various designs, one of which was the ram's head on the small coin at the top. The colony was extremely prosperous, and from about B.C. 350, its silver coins were widely used by the Celtic peoples of Gaul and northern Italy.

Prow of Roman galley

Back

Front

CELTIC WARRIOR
This lifelike portrait of a Gaulish chief and his war chariot appear on the front and back of a silver coin of the Roman Republic. It was made in about B.C. 48, soon after Julius Caesar's conquest of Gaul.

ROMAN GAUL COIN
The letters "CI V" on this coin stand for "Colonia Julia Viennensis", the "Colony of Julius Caesar at Vienne". Vienne is in the south of France and is where this coin was made around B.C. 36.

Louis XIV chose the sun as his emblem because he saw himself as the all-powerful centre of the universe!

SILVER DENIER AND GROS
Charlemagne (742–814) issued this denier (left). The denier was introduced by his father, Pepin, the first king of France. It was virtually the only denomination used in France until the introduction of the silver gros (right) by King Louis IX in 1266.

PHILIPPE "LE BEL"
Philippe IV, who reigned from 1285–1314, was known as "le bel", the handsome. This splendid gold coin deserves the same title! Until the time of Philippe, gold coins were scarce.

"LUD" is the abbreviation of "Ludivicus", the Latin form of "Louis"

SILVER ECU
From the time of Francis I (1515–1547), portraits of the kings of France appeared on coins. The famous king of France, Louis XIV (the "Sun King"), appears on this écu (left). The European Economic Community has recently revived the name ECU (European Currency Unit) for its new common currency unit.

Loi du 23 Mai 1793. | Série 621 | L'an 2ème de la République.

Domaines nationaux. Assignat de cinquante sols, payable au porteur.

The denomination "sol" was popularly known as "sou"

First Republic, 1792–1804

Second Republic, 1848–1852

Third Republic, 1871–1940

FIVE MARIANNES
From 1793, the main design of French Republican coinage has been a female head representing the Republic. The image became popularly known as "Marianne". She is normally shown wearing the cap of liberty or a wreath. Many different versions have been used; the five here are found on coins of the five Republics.

Fourth Republic, 1945-1958

Fifth Republic, 1958–present day

REVOLUTIONARY PAPER MONEY
From 1790 until 1793, the French Revolution was funded by issues of paper money known as "assignats" (left). Coins like those on the right continued to be issued using the pre-revolutionary denominations, but the designs were changed to reflect the political situation. The franc became the main unit of currency in 1795.

Five-livre coin of Louis XVI issued in 1792, the year before his execution on the guillotine

Royal portrait is replaced by the figures of Hercules, Liberty, and Equality on this five-franc coin of 1795

Napoleon Bonaparte's portrait appeared on coins from 1802 when he was made Consul of the Republic. He became Emperor in 1804

MONEY TO BURN
Because far too many "assignats" were issued, the notes became worthless. In 1796, the printing presses were destroyed, and the notes burnt.

Today's money

Space for watermark

LOCAL PAPER MONEY
During the First World War, and for a few years after, most small change was issued locally. Both coins and notes, like this 50-centimes note of Grenoble, were issued by local trade associations.

CHAMBRE DE COMMERCE DE GRENOBLE
DÉLIBÉRATION DU 8 NOVEMBRE 1917
50 CENTIMES
CETTE COUPURE, ÉCHANGEABLE CONTRE DES BILLETS DE LA BANQUE DE FRANCE, DEVRA ÊTRE PRÉSENTÉE AU REMBOURSEMENT AVANT LE 9 NOVEMBRE 1922 SAUF DÉCISION PROROGEANT CE DELAI

COMMEMORATIVE COIN
Commemorative coins are frequently issued for general circulation. This 1988 franc celebrates the 30th anniversary of the election of Charles de Gaulle as President.

10F   5F   2F

1F   50c

20c   10c   5c

500 BANQUE DE FRANCE 500

BANQUE de FRANCE

BANQUE de FRANCE 20 VINGT FRANCS

See pages 62–63

Germany

THE MARK, DIVIDED INTO 100 PFENNIGS, is the currency unit of both parts of Germany – the Federal Republic in the west and the Democratic Republic in the east. The mark was introduced in 1871 when the German Empire was formed by Wilhelm I, King of Prussia. Before it became the main unit of currency, the mark was used as a weight. The main currencies were the thaler, the gulden, and the ducat. The pfennig, however, has a longer history, and was the name used for German silver coins of the 11th century. Before the Empire was established, the German kingdoms, states, and cities each had their own currency system. Similar coinage systems existed in the neighbouring areas of Poland, Czechoslovakia, Austria, and Switzerland.

This engraving shows a Mint Master weighing out coins in the 14th century

ROMAN GOLD
This large gold coin was made at the mint in Trier to reward soldiers serving the Roman emperor, Constantius I. Britannia kneels before him as he is crowned by Victory, a Roman goddess.

Conrad II, King of Saxony (1024–1039)

SILVER PFENNIGS
Early pfennigs, like the one at the top, used French and English designs, but during the 12th century, many original German designs appeared on broader, thinner versions. The coin on the left is an issue of Emperor Frederick I Barbarossa (1152–1190), and the coin on the right was issued by Otto I of Brandenburg (1157–1184).

In this 15th-century Swiss drawing, you can see coinmakers minting small silver pfennigs

Coin issued in Rhenish Palatine showing St. John the Baptist

Coin issued in Trier showing St. Peter

Coin issued in Basel showing the Virgin Mary

GOLD GULDEN
Gold coins began to be issued in quantity during the 14th century. They were the same size as Italian florins (p. 36).

Thaler of Count Stephen of Slick, 1519

Thaler of Johan Wilhelm, Duke of Saxony, 1569

SILVER THALERS
During the 15th century, the discovery of large silver mines in Joachimsthal in Bohemia (now called Austria) led to the issue of new, large, silver coins. These were called Joachimsthalers, "thalers" for short. The word "dollar" is the English version of this name. The silver from the Bohemian mines was exported throughout western Europe.

The horse leaping over the silver mines is the symbol of Luneburg

Four-thaler coin of Christian Ludwig, Duke of Brunswick-Luneburg, 1662

The arm of God crowns the horse

FREDERICK THE GREAT OF PRUSSIA
Frederick, the Philospher King (1740–1786), reorganized his coinage system so that it was based on the thaler and the pfennig. This gold coin struck at Berlin in 1750 was worth 10 thalers.

REICHSKASSENSCHEIN
GESETZ VOM 31. APRIL 1874.
FÜNF MARK.
BERLIN, DEN 31. OKTOBER 1904.
REICHSSCHULDENVERWALTUNG

FIVE-MARK NOTE
When Wilhelm I of Prussia became the Emperor (Kaiser) of Germany in 1871, the German monetary system was unified, with the mark as the main unit of currency. The former thaler was equal to five marks.

Coins made of iron

STACKS OF MONEY
During 1923, the German monetary system descended into chaos and banknotes became worthless. As well as using notes as wallpaper, parents gave bundles to children to play with!

Zehn-Pfennig
Gutschein der Stadt Wetzlar

200.000.000
Die Stadtgemeinde Köln haftet für die Einlösung. Köln, 14 Sept. 1923. Der Oberbürgerm. *Adenauer.*
Gutschein der Stadt Köln
Zweihundert Millionen Mark
REIHE A · № 401527

M. DUMONT SCHAUBERG KÖLN

LOCAL MONEY
During and after the First World War, small-change coins and notes were issued by local authorities.

ZERO MADNESS
Because the mark became more and more worthless after the First World War people needed more marks to buy goods. To keep up with this, banks issued notes with high denominations, like this Cologne 200 million mark note. Bank clerks went insane dealing with the ever-increasing number of zeros!

EAST GERMAN 10-PFENNIG
The two halves of Germany, East and West, have used separate currencies since 1948. The backs of the East German coins have designs representing labour and agriculture. The back of this 10-pfennig coin displays a cogged wheel of industry and an ear of corn to represent agriculture.

DEUTSCHLAND 10 PFENNIG

Design showing cogged wheel and ear of corn

Today's money

Banknote
DEUTSCHE MARK
100 HUNDERT DEUTSCHE MARK

10pfg · 50pfg · 1DM · 2DM · 5DM

See pages 62–63

Netherlands and Belgium

Detail from "The Moneylender and his wife" by the Flemish painter, Quentin Massys

THE MODERN CURRENCIES of the Netherlands and Belgium were established when they became kingdoms. In 1815, the Kingdom of the United Netherlands – which at that time included Belgium– kept its former gulden currency, but reorganized it as a decimal system divided into 100 cents. When the Belgian kingdom became independent from the Netherlands in 1830, it adopted the franc from France, the country that had ruled both countries during the earlier Napoleonic period. Coinage had originally been introduced by the Celts into this area in the second century B.C. It then developed further under Roman, German, French, Spanish, and British influence. From the 13th century, the Netherlands and Belgium were the centre of international trade, and many foreign coins circulated there (pp. 20–21).

BELGIAN GOLD
This is an example of the earliest Belgian coins made by the Celtic tribe called the Nervii. These coins have also been found in the Netherlands.

MEROVINGIAN GOLD
The mint of Duurstede is named on the earliest Dutch coins. It is spelt DORESTAT on this gold coin of the Merovingian kings.

Gold lion of Philip le Bon, Duke of Burgundy (1419–1467)

Dutch gold ducat of Rudolph, Bishop of Utrecht (1423–1455)

Belgian silver gros of Adolf, Bishop of Liège (1313–1344)

LOCAL COINS
From the 11th to 16th centuries, many local gold and silver coins were issued in Belgium and the Netherlands. The largest issues were by the Dukes of Burgundy, but local religious leaders, nobles, and towns also issued their own coins.

SIEGE MONEY
These coins are emergency issues of cities involved in the revolt of the Dutch United Provinces, which began in 1568 against their Spanish rulers.

Lion of Holland countermark added to Spanish coins by order of William Prince of Orange in 1573

Cardboard coin made when Leiden was besieged by the Spanish army (1574)

Bundle of arrows represents the Dutch United Provinces

SPANISH OR FREE?
The mint of the Duchy of Gelderland produced both these Dutch gold coins. The coin on the left was issued by the Spanish king, Philip II, in 1560. The coin on the right was struck by independent Gelderland in the name of the United Provinces in 1616.

Silver coin made by the Spanish governor of Amsterdam while under attack by the Dutch (1578)

EARL OF LEICESTER
The English Earl of Leicester, acting for Elizabeth I, Queen of England, supported the Dutch revolt against Spain. In 1586, he attempted to reorganize the Dutch coinage system.

Isabella and her husband, Archduke Albert of Austria

DOUBLE SOVEREIGN
In 1598, Philip II of Spain handed over his Dutch and Belgian possessions to his daughter Isabella and her husband, Archduke Albert of Austria. This gold coin was made at the Brussels mint in 1618.

THE PORT OF AMSTERDAM
During the 16th century, many wealthy merchants lived in Amsterdam as it was one of the busiest trading cities in the world. The town is cut by some 40 canals, which are crossed by about 400 bridges.

TRADE AND EMPIRE

This Dutch "daalder"(Dutch version of "dollar") coin copied the Spanish "piece of eight" from Mexico

A variety of forms of money was made for the Dutch empire established during the 17th century. This silver daalder was made in Amsterdam in 1601 for trade with the Far East, and the copper bar coin was made in Ceylon in 1785. The gulden note was issued by the Javasche Bank in the Dutch East Indies in 1920.

THE RIVER CONGO
The only trade route into the Belgian Congo was along the great Congo river.

French coin

Flemish coin

BILINGUAL COINS
Because Belgium has two official languages, French and Flemish, two separate sets of coins are now issued. Previously, some coins had both languages on the same coin.

CONGO FRANC
In 1885, the Belgian king became ruler of a part of Central Africa which became known as the Belgian Congo (now called Zaire). This cupro-nickel franc (1922) was made in Brussels for use in the Congo.

ANTWERP SIEGE COIN
During the Napoleonic Wars, Belgium and the Netherlands were ruled by France. The N on this copper coin stands for Napoleon, whose supporters were besieged in Antwerp in 1814.

BELGIAN WAR MONEY
During the First World War, special emergency banknotes were used in occupied Belgium. They could only be changed into the official notes of the National Bank of Belgium three months after the end of the war. This one-franc note was issued in 1917.

Leopold I of Belgium

Willem III of the Netherlands

ROYAL GOLD
After the defeat of Napoleon in 1814, both Belgium and the Netherlands were united as the Kingdom of the United Netherlands. In 1830, Belgium became a separate kingdom. Both kingdoms issued coins with royal portraits.

Today's money: Belgium
Reproduced with the written permission of the National Bank of Belgium

Today's money: Netherlands

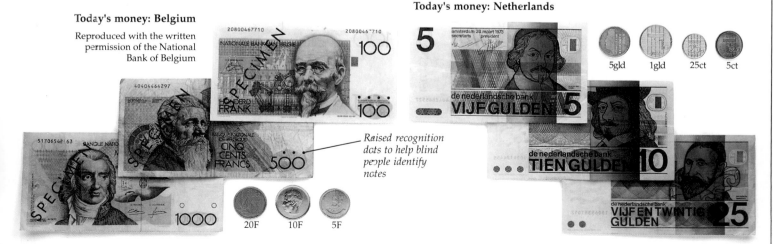

Raised recognition dots to help blind people identify notes

5gld   1gld   25ct   5ct

20F   10F   5F

See pages 62–63

Italy

THE LIRA WAS ESTABLISHED as Italy's national currency from the mid 19th century when Vittorio Emanuele II became King of Italy. The word lira comes from the Latin word *libra*, the unit of weight used to set the value of early Roman copper money. Before they used coins, the Romans made payments with cattle and weighed lumps of copper. They got the idea for coins during the third century B.C. from the Greek cities of southern Italy and Sicily where coins had been in use for over 200 years. Early Roman coins were versions of Greek coins or weighed copper money with Greek designs added to them (pp. 10–11). Italian cities such as Pavia, Genoa, Venice, Florence, and Amalfi dominated European trade for centuries. Italian gold ducats were used and imitated throughout Europe and the Eastern Mediterranean countries.

In the time of Augustus, soldiers of the Roman army were paid 225 denarii a year

GREEK SILVER
Many Greek settlements in southern Italy issued coins from the 6th century B.C. This example was minted at Tarento during the 4th century.

X, the Roman numeral 10, showed that this silver denarius was worth 10 of the copper one-pound coins

I, the Roman numeral 1, showed that this coin represented one pound (libra) of copper

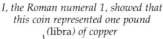

EARLY ROMAN MONEY
Rome's first money took the form of cast copper lumps, like the one above, weighed out in payments. During the 3rd century, coin-shaped cast copper lumps (left) were used instead (pp. 10–11). A silver coin (denarius), showing the head of the goddess Roma, was issued at the same time.

Silver denarius of Julius Caesar, B.C. 44

Gold aureus of Augustus, B.C. 27 – A.D. 14

Bronze sestertius of Nero, A.D. 54–68

ROMAN EMPIRE COINS
Silver, gold, and bronze coins were issued by most Roman emperors. Their portrait was normally the main design. The emperors often used these coins to make themselves known to their subjects. It was a good way to show people what they looked like, what they did, and what their titles were. Remember, there were no newspapers or televisions in those days!

BARBARIAN COIN
You can just see the twin founders of Rome – Romulus and Remus – and the wolf who helped look after them on this bronze coin issued by the Ostrogoth (Barbarian) conquerors of the city in the 6th century.

ANYONE FOR THE GAMES?
The most famous standing monument of the Roman Empire, the Colosseum was pictured on coins in the year A.D. 80 when it was completed. It was here that The Games were held, when men (gladiators) and animals fought to the death to provide entertainment for the bloodthirsty emperors and citizens.

This 20-"ducat" coin is from the "duchy" of Venice

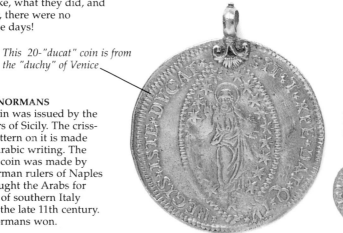

ARABS AND NORMANS
This gold coin was issued by the Arab rulers of Sicily. The criss-cross pattern on it is made up of Arabic writing. The copper coin was made by the Norman rulers of Naples who fought the Arabs for control of southern Italy during the late 11th century. The Normans won.

DUCAT AND FLORIN
During the 13th century, the Italian cities of Venice and Florence began to issue gold coins called ducats or sequins in Venice, and florins in Florence. The large coin on the left is a 20-ducat piece from Venice. The smaller piece is a Florentine florin. The first German gold coins were modelled on the florin (p. 32).

Austrian coin

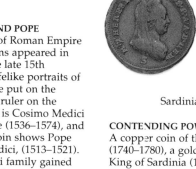

Sardinian coin

Spanish coin

PRINCE AND POPE
A revival of Roman Empire coin designs appeared in Italy in the late 15th century; lifelike portraits of rulers were put on the coins. The ruler on the silver coin is Cosimo Medici of Florence (1536–1574), and the gold coin shows Pope Leo X, Medici, (1513–1521). The Medici family gained great wealth as merchants and bankers, and were extremely influential in Florence.

CONTENDING POWERS
A copper coin of the Austrian Empress, Maria Theresa (1740–1780), a gold coin of Vittorio Amadeo of Savoy, King of Sardinia (1773–1796), and a silver coin of Ferdinand IV, the Spanish king of the Two Sicilies (1759–1825), represent the three main powers struggling for control of Italy during the 18th century.

ROMAN "ASSIGNAT" *right*
In 1798, the states ruled by the Pope rejected his authority and together formed the Roman Republic. Like the French Republic that inspired it, the Roman Republic also issued "assignats" (p. 31).

LIRE NOTE *below*
The lira became the national currency of Italy in 1861 when Vittorio Emanuele II became King of Italy. This 30-lire note was issued in 1884 by a Sardinian bank.

Year 7 of the French Republic

ITALIAN BANKERS
It was in northern Italy, particularly in the area known as Lombardy, that the practice of banking first began during the 14th century. This was the beginning of modern commercial banking as we know it today.

Today's money

L.500   L.200

L.100   L.50

1000

POLITICAL COIN
This 1923 two-lire coin of King Vittorio Emanuele III used the Fascist emblem (a bundle of sticks and an axe) as its main design. As a protest, an anti-Fascist user of the coin stamped the Communist emblem of a hammer and sickle on it.

SMALL CHANGE
A shortage of small-denomination coins during the 1970s forced shopkeepers to give telephone tokens and sweets as change.

10000 LIRE DIECIMILA

5000 LIRE CINQUEMILA

BANCA D'ITALIA

D'ITALIA

50000 LIRE CINQUANTAMILA

100000

37

See pages 62–63

Spain and Portugal

Spanish and Portuguese galleons were often loaded with treasure

IN 1492, CHRISTOPHER COLUMBUS set out from Spain to open up a westward route to the East, and found the Americas. Six years later, Vasco da Gama from Portugal opened the sea route around Africa to India. These two events dramatically changed the history of money. They led to the issue of European-style coins in the Americas, Africa, and eventually Asia, and also brought to Europe vast amounts of gold and silver from those continents. Spain shipped into Europe and Asia millions of silver "pieces of eight" from Mexico, Peru, and Bolivia in South America. Portugal supplied Europe with gold taken from Africa, India, China, and Brazil. Spain's peseta, introduced in 1869, got its name from the popular term for a small silver coin. The modern Portuguese escudo is a more recent creation; it was first issued in 1915.

Greek coin from Emporium, B.C. 250

Carthaginian coin, Spain, B.C. 210

Spanish Celtic coin, c. B.C. 100

Coin of Carthaginian settlement at Salacia in Portugal, c. B.C. 100

ANCIENT COINS
Greek colonists had introduced coinage into Spain and Portugal by the 4th century B.C. Their main mint was at Emporium (now called Ampurias) in northeast Spain. Later, Carthaginian, Celtic, and Roman coins were also issued.

Spanish Roman copper coin from Saragossa, c. A.D. 20

Moorish gold coin

Visigoth gold coin

Coin from Castile, copying a Moorish design

Portuguese gold coin

MOORISH GOLD
In 711, an Arab-led Moorish army conquered the Visigoths in Spain and began to issue their own coins. The Islamic designs on Moorish coins were copied on the earliest coins of the Christian kings of Castile and Portugal, who had driven the Moors out of Spain by the 15th century.

Roman aqueduct of Segovia, the mark of the Segovian mint

NEW WORLDS
The search for gold took Columbus to the Americas, and Vasco da Gama to India. The gold they found was used to make coins like the piece (top left) of Ferdinand and Isabella of Spain (1479–1504), and the piece (top right) of John III of Portugal (1521–1557).

Silver "pieces of eight"

Robinson Crusoe

Gold doubloon

"I got all my cargo on shore . . . I found there were three great bags of pieces of eight . . . and in one of them, wrapped up in paper, six doubloons of gold".

SPANISH EMPIRE
The Spanish conquerors of the Americas were quick to exploit the rich gold sources and silver mines they found in Mexico, Bolivia, and Peru. These crudely made coins, silver "pieces of eight" and gold doubloons, were loaded on to treasure ships bound for Europe. These ships often fell prey to pirates!

PORTUGUESE EMPIRE
Portugal's empire in the Indian Ocean was based on trade. The tin coin (left) was made in 1511 for local use at the port of Malacca in Malaya. In 1693, gold was discovered in Brazil, and was made into coins like the 1725 Portuguese coin (right) in Rio de Janeiro, Brazil. The coins were then exported.

CONQUISTADORS VERSUS INDIANS
Spanish conquistadors fought the Inca and Aztec peoples of America for their supplies of gold and silver.

50-reales coin made in Segovia from Spanish American silver

Original VIII (eight) stamp

MONEY TROUBLES
The flow of silver and gold into Spain made it the richest country in the world, but it wasted the money on war. Prices went up and copper coins had to be revalued. This copper coin was revalued from eight maravedis to 12 maravedis in 1652.

XII (twelve) stamp revaluing coin

Joseph Napoleon

Ferdinand VII

Duke of Wellington

TWO SPANISH KINGS
In 1808, there were two new kings crowned in Spain: the legitimate heir, Ferdinand VII, and Napoleon's brother, Joseph. A British army, led by the future Duke of Wellington, drove the French usurper out. Both kings issued their own coins, but the British army used its own money, including tokens showing Wellington's portrait.

PORTUGUESE WAR NOTE
After the Napoleonic War, civil war continued in Portugal. This 1805 note was reissued in 1828 by the usurper, Miguel I.

Today's money: Spain

SPANISH CIVIL WAR
This note was issued by the Spanish Republican government during the Civil War (1936–1939). After the War, coins were issued showing the portrait of General Franco, victorious commander of the anti-Republican forces.

200 ptas
100 ptas
25 ptas

Today's money: Portugal

"LIBERTY AND DEMOCRACY"
These words are inscribed on this Portuguese coin celebrating the restoration of democratic government in 1974.

20 esc
10 esc
2.5 esc

Greece and Turkey

"AS RICH AS CROESUS"
This saying refers to the wealth of Croesus, King of Lydia (c. B.C. 560–547). He is thought to have issued the coin above, one of the first gold coins in the world.

ROYAL IMAGES
Greek kings are to be seen on these two silver coins; Philip II of Macedonia (B.C. 359–336) on horseback (above), and Antiochus I of Syria (B.C. 281–261) on a coin from southern Turkey (right).

TODAY'S COINS ALL HAVE THEIR ORIGIN in the Ancient Greek versions of the coins first made in Ancient Turkey (pp. 10–11). The Ancient Greeks gave coins their distinctive round shape with designs on both sides. Since then, Greece and Turkey have had many different rulers – Greek, Persian, Roman, Byzantine, Turkish, French, Italian, British, Russian, and German – who have all issued coins of their own. The current money of both countries, the Greek drachma and the Turkish lira, are of quite recent origin. The drachma, which takes its name from a coin of Ancient Greece, began in 1831 when Greece became independent. The lira, first issued as paper money in 1930, represented the renaming of the Turkish pound (livre).

FLYING PIG
The design and inscription on this silver coin identify it as a 5th-century B.C. issue of the city of Ialysus on the Greek island of Rhodes.

Greek writing was used in the Byzantine Empire

BYZANTINE GOLD
The Byzantine emperor, Alexius II (1297–1330), issued coins like this one in Constantinople (now Istanbul), Turkey and Thessalonika, Greece.

Coin issued for Mark Antony before the battle of Actium (B.C. 31)

SULEIMAN THE MAGNIFICENT
Suleiman, the most powerful of all the Ottoman sultans (1494–1566) issued the gold coin below. His reign was noted for its military power.

Seated warrior is holding a severed head

ROMAN COINS
The Romans issued many coins in the parts of their empire now known as Greece and Turkey. The gold coin (above right) is a Greek issue for Mark Antony. The large bronze coin from Turkey features the Roman Emperor, Caracalla.

THE CRUSADES
The small silver coin (top) was issued by a French crusader who ruled as the Duke of Athens (1280–1287). The copper coins were made by rival forces fighting for eastern Turkey. The lion's face coin (centre) was issued by the Christian Armenian kings of Cilicia (1187–1218), and the seated warrior coin (bottom), by the Turkish rulers of Mardin.

Silver aqche of Thessalonika (Salonika), 1574

Paper kurus of the Ottoman Imperial Bank, 1877

Gold altin of Istanbul, 1520

Tughra emblem

Silver kurus of Istanbul, 1769

THE SULTAN'S MONEY
The Turkish Ottoman sultans ruled both Greece and Turkey. They issued their pictureless coins throughout their empire, which stretched from Algeria to Iraq, and from Hungary to Yemen. The knotted emblem (known as a tughra) on the large silver coin and the note is the official "signature" of the sultans.

Venetian copper soldo of the 18th century

COINS OF CORFU
Corfu and the other Ionian islands were for a long time the only parts of Greece to escape Turkish Ottoman rule. From 1402 until 1797 they were ruled by Venice, but they then passed briefly through the hands of France, Russia, Turkey, and France again until 1815 when Britain took control. In 1863, they finally became part of Greece.

Russian copper gazetta, 1801

The phoenix, symbol of rebirth, taken from a Greek banknote

Otto I gold coin

INDEPENDENT GREECE
In 1828, Greece, the "mother of democracy", achieved independence from Turkish rule. The first coins, like this copper 10-lepton of 1831, were issued by the Greek Republic. In 1831, Greece became a kingdom under Otto I of Bavaria, whose portrait appears on the gold 20-drachma coin.

Greek Republic copper coin

British copper obol, 1819

CORFU CRICKET
During the British occupation of Corfu, the British troops missed their traditional game of cricket, so they built a cricket pitch in Corfu town. The venerable game of cricket is still played there regularly, but by the Greeks, not the British.

National Bank of Greece one-drachma note, 1885

ISLAND MONEY
The Greek island of Thasos remained under Turkish rule until 1914. This Turkish copper 40-para coin was countermarked by the Greek community in Thasos in 1893.

NEW COINS, OLD DESIGNS
The second Greek Republic (1925–1935) used Ancient Greek coin designs on its new issues. The design of this two-drachma coin is the head of Athena, copied from an ancient coin of Corinth.

Today's money: Greece

50dr

20dr

5dr

1dr

TURKISH REPUBLIC
In 1923, Ottoman rule in Turkey ceased, and it became a republic under the leadership of Kamel Ataturk. His portrait appears on this 100-kurus (one-lira) coin which was issued in 1934.

Today's money: Turkey

100L   50L   10L   1L

LOCAL GREEK NOTE
During the Second World War, many locally issued notes were in use. This 5000-drachma note is from Zagora.

41

See pages 62–63

Denmark and Norway

Coin of King Cnut (1019–1035) from his mint at Lund

Norwegian penny of Viking King Olaf Kyrre (1067–1093)

SILVER PENNIES
English designs were copied on early Danish and Norwegian silver pennies. An example of the Norwegian coin above was recently found at a Viking settlement in North America.

BEFORE DENMARK AND NORWAY had their own coins, the Vikings introduced French, German, English, and Islamic coins that they had captured as booty or acquired in trade. During the 10th and 11th centuries, the Danish and Norwegian kings began to issue their own coins, with designs copied from English silver pennies. Today, Denmark and Norway both use the krone, divided into 100 øre, as their currency. The same denominations are used in Sweden (pp. 44–45). These three separate currencies were introduced in 1873 as part of a common Scandinavian system. The krone ("crown") had originally been a silver coin with a crown design issued by the kings of Denmark and Norway in the 17th and 18th centuries. The øre was of Swedish origin.

CNUT RULES THE WAVES!
According to legend, King Cnut of Denmark and England tried to prove his power by commanding the tide to stop; he failed. Cnut issued English-style pennies for use in both kingdoms.

KING OF DENMARK AND NORWAY
King Christian IV (1588–1648) was king of both Denmark and Norway, but he issued separate coins for each kingdom. The silver coin on the left is Danish, and the one on the right, Norwegian.

ROYAL GIFTS
Square coins, called klippe, were often issued in Denmark during the 16th and 17th centuries. Square coins were first used as emergency issues in war, as they were quicker to make than round ones. These two klippe are special coins that were made for the king to give away as presents.

The letter 'C' is the initial of the king who issued this klippe, Christian V

Pillars and globe design copied from a "piece of eight" (p. 21)

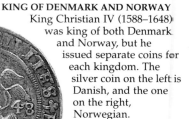

The Lapp reindeer herdsmen of northern Norway used reindeer and furs as payments

TRADE COINS
This silver coin, copied from a Spanish American "piece of eight", was made in 1777 for the Danish Asiatic Society to use in China. The picture on the small gold coin (1726) shows Christiansborg, a Danish settlement in West Africa where the gold used for the coin came from.

MARKS AND SKILLINGS
During the 18th century, the Danish and Norwegian monetary system was based on the mark, which was divided into 16 skillings. This silver krone of 1723 was worth four marks. 64 of the copper skillings (far right) made a krone.

A Viking war ship

The lion with axe design was used on Norwegian coins. There are four on these pages

PAPER AND SILVER DALERS

In 1813, the Danish government introduced a currency based on a daler of 96 skilling. This daler note was issued in Christiania (the old name for Oslo, Norway) by the Danish Royal Bank of Copenhagen. The daler continued to be used in Norway after it came under the control of the King of Sweden in 1814. This silver daler was issued in 1823.

Dolphin and grain symbolise fishing and agriculture

SCANDINAVIAN MONEY

In 1873, a unified currency system was created for Denmark, Norway, and Sweden. The same denominations were issued by each country, but different designs were used. The 20-kroner and 5-øre coins above are from Denmark (top), and Norway (bottom). For Sweden's versions, see p. 45.

PAPER KRONE

During the First World War, and for a few years after, local emergency paper money was issued in Denmark. This example was made by the Odense Credit Bank.

Today's money: Denmark

Today's money: Norway

1kr   25øre

10kr   1kr   50øre

EMERGENCY COINS

During the Second World War, there was a shortage of copper, because it was used to make shell cases. This meant that both Denmark and Norway had to use different metals to make their coins. Norway issued coins made of iron (left), and Denmark issued coins made from aluminium (right), and zinc.

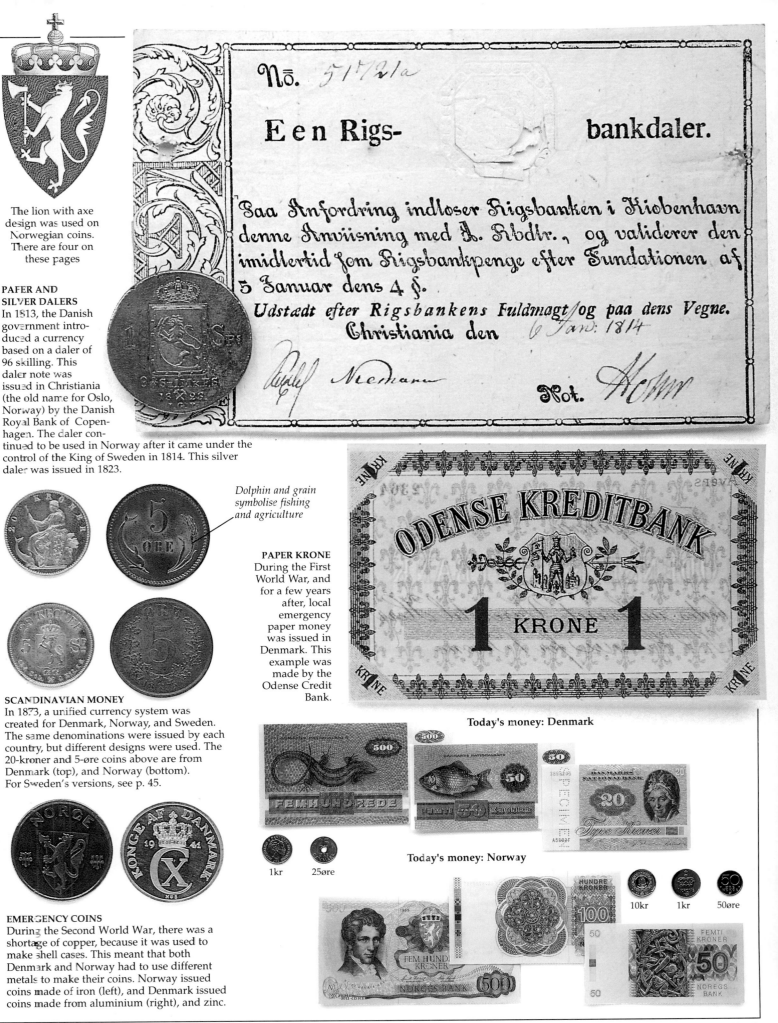

See pages 62–63

Sweden and Finland

As well as issuing Europe's first paper money, Sweden issued the biggest coins ever made – copper plate money. These huge rectangular coins could weigh up to about 19 kg (42 lb)! Today, Sweden's money is not so strange; it is based on the krona, divided into 100 öre. Until 1809, Finland used Swedish money as it was ruled by the Swedish crown. However, in that year Finland came under Russian control and the rouble and kopek were used. Today's markka and penni were also introduced by the Russians.

SWEDISH COPIES
The coin (left) is a copy of an Islamic coin. The penny (right) was made by visiting English coinmakers.

ONE-SIDED COINS
Silver pennies with a design on one side only were made in the 13th century. The M (top) is for King Magnus of Sweden; the A (right) is for Abo, the old name for the Finnish city, Turku.

DALERS, DUCATS, AND ÖRE
In 1534, Gustav I Vasa (1523–1560) introduced Sweden's first silver daler (left). This also circulated in Finland, part of his kingdom. Gustav II Adolf (1611–1632) introduced Sweden's first copper coinage, square pieces denominated in öre (centre). Swedish rule extended into Germany, and Gustav Adolf II issued gold ducats for his subjects there. His daughter, Kristina (1634–1654), is shown on the silver daler (right).

Massive man-powered drop hammers were used to stamp the designs on to plate money

PLATE MONEY
Sweden first issued huge copper coins called plate money during Kristina's reign. There were rich copper mines at Avesta and Falun (the copper mountain at Falun is shown on the token above). Plate money was very heavy; the square one-daler piece (right) weighs almost 2 kg (4 lb), so paper money, like this cheque worth 288 dalers, was used instead.

DALER TOKENS

In 1717, the Swedish government ran out of money because of a costly war with Russia. It issued both paper and small copper dalers instead of the plate money. The copper dalers were decorated with pictures of Roman gods. The dalers here show Mercury, Jupiter, Saturn, and Mars.

Paper daler

Copper dalers

Notes were only valid if all three signatures appeared

Russian Imperial two-headed eagle

This design is taken from a Finnish banknote; the name of the Bank of Finland is written in Swedish, Finnish, and Russian

RUSSIAN FINLAND

In 1809, Sweden lost control of Finland to Russia. The Russians introduced into Finland their own roubles and kopeks. The 20-kopek note (right) was issued in 1840. Finland was given its own currency in 1864 when coins denominated in markkaa, divided into 100 penniä, were introduced. The gold coin (above right) is a 20-markkaa piece, and the copper coin below it, a 10-penniä.

COMMON COINS

Sweden's money has been denominated in kronor and öre since 1873 when, along with Denmark and Norway, it reorganized its currency to form a common system. The öre was already in use in Sweden. This 5-öre coin was issued in 1857, but the gold 20-kronor was issued in 1876.

INDEPENDENT FINLAND

Finland has a different coinage system to the other Scandinavian countries. When it became independent in 1917, it kept the currency system introduced by the Russians.

5Kr

1Kr

50öre

Today's money: Sweden

Today's money: Finland

1MK

20p

1p

See pages 62–63

The Royal Mint was located in or near the Tower of London for almost 1,000 years

The United Kingdom

CELTIC GOLD
This Celtic coin (c. A.D. 10–40) names a famous Ancient British king, Cunobelin, king of the Catuvellauni tribe.

ALL THE REGIONS of the United Kingdom of Great Britain – England, Scotland, Northern Ireland, Wales, the Isle of Man, and the Channel Isles – now use a monetary system based on the pound sterling divided into 100 pennies. Before 1971, the pound sterling was divided into 240 pennies, 12 of which made a shilling. Different forms of paper money circulate in each region, except England and Wales, which share Bank of England notes. Different coins are issued for the Isle of Man and the Channel Islands of Guernsey and Jersey. The other regions use British coins made by the Royal Mint in Llantrisant, Wales. Celts and Romans introduced coins into Britain, and Britain has since been responsible for introducing its own money to many parts of the world, largely through trade and war. The pound sterling is still one of the world's most important currencies.

ROMAN MINT
The Roman mint at London (Londinium) made this bronze coin for the Emperor Maximian. The name of the mint, "LON", is at the bottom of the coin.

SAXON AND VIKING PENNIES
The Anglo-Saxons introduced the silver penny; the coin (left) shows the Saxon king Alfred the Great. The coin (right) names Eric Bloodaxe, the Viking King of York.

Silver sixpence

MACHINE-MADE MONEY
The silver sixpence of Elizabeth I (above) was the first to be made in 1566 with a screw-press coining machine like the one in the picture at the Tower mint (above left).

Scottish kings always faced to the side on sterling pennies

Punch marks to test that coin was solid gold (p. 19)

STERLING SILVER PENNIES
King Edward I introduced a new silver penny, the "sterling", in 1279. His new coins were so frequently used in trade that many foreign copies were made of them. These coins are sterlings of Edward I (left), and Robert Bruce, King of Scotland (right).

GROAT AND NOBLE
As trade expanded during the 14th century, the standard silver penny was joined by several new, more valuable coins. The silver groat (left), was worth four pennies, and the gold noble (right), 80 pennies.

18TH-CENTURY SMALL CHANGE
Local small change reappeared in the late 18th century when the government failed to issue copper coins. Local traders responded by issuing their own copper tokens. The Welsh druid halfpenny (top) was made by a Welsh copper mining company; the Lady Godiva coin (centre) was issued in Coventry.

"The Queen's Head" public house, London

SMALL CHANGE
During the 17th century, a shortage of small change prompted traders and innkeepers to issue brass farthings (quarter penny) and halfpennies.

COPPER HALFPENNY
Britain's first official copper halfpenny of 1672 had the image of Britannia on the back.

LADY GODIVA
According to legend, Lady Godiva rode naked through the streets of Coventry to persuade her husband to lower the heavy taxes. The only person to peek at her as she rode became known as "Peeping Tom".

The thick rim of the 1797 steam press coins earned them the nickname "cartwheels"

GOLD SOVEREIGN

The first British pound coin, (worth 240 silver pennies), was introduced by King Henry VII in 1489. This example (c. 1545) was struck at the Southwark mint for King Henry VIII, whose large figure is seen seated on the throne.

GOLD UNITE

A new pound coin was introduced by King James I in 1604. This one (1650) was made during the English Civil War when England was ruled by Parliament after James' son, King Charles I, had been executed.

GOLD "GUINEA"

This machine-made gold pound (1663) depicts King Charles II. The elephant at the bottom shows that it was made with gold from Africa's Guinea Coast.

GOLD SOVEREIGN

A new gold pound coin was issued during King George III's reign (1738–1820). It was called a sovereign, like the first gold pound coin.

PAPER GUINEA
Paper money (pp. 12–13) became popular in Britain during the 18th century. This Scottish guinea note of 1777 was the first to be printed in three colours.

Queen Victoria liked to give £5 coins like this one as a souvenir to her court visitors

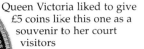

The 1849 florin

DECIMAL COINS
The first attempt at decimalization (division into units of 10) was made in 1849 with the introduction of a two-shilling coin, the florin, which was a tenth of a pound. This became a ten-pence coin after full decimalization in 1971.

Today's equivalent 10-pence coin

Today's money

£1 50p 20p 10p

5p 2p 1p

50p £1 5p
Isle of Man Jersey Guernsey

WARTIME SIXPENCE NOTE
The Island of Jersey issued its own locally designed and printed notes during the Second World War.

See pages 62– 63

Canada

COINS AND BANKNOTES were first introduced into Canada by British and French settlers, but the native peoples continued to use their own traditional means of payment such as beads and blankets. The settlers preferred to use furs and grain as money, or to make their own! The dollar and cent currency used today was introduced during the 1850s. Forms of the British and French currency systems were in use before that but, as in the USA, the Spanish dollar was the main coin in circulation. The Dominion of Canada, established in 1867, adopted the dollar as its official currency in 1868.

FRENCH CANADIAN COIN
Canada's first coins were made in Paris for French settlers on the orders of Louis XIV of France. This silver piece was made in 1670.

"BEAVER" MONEY
The Hudson Bay (Trading) Company issued its own paper money like this one-shilling note, but the traders used beaver skins as money. It also issued this brass token for one beaver skin.

No. 3214 ONE SHILLING Sterly 1845.
Hudsons Bay Company.
Promise to pay the Bearer on Demand
the Sum of ONE SHILLING for YORK FACTORY, in RUPERTS LAND
in a Bill of Exchange payable Sixty days after Sight at the
Hudsons Bay House, London. 3214
LONDON, the 1st day of May 1845. For the Governor & Company
of Adventurers of England, trading into Hudsons Bay
No. 3214 A Barclay SECRETARY.
Issued at York Factory, the 4th day of March 1846 by
GOVERNOR.
Ent Accountant.

PROVINCIAL TOKENS
British sterling was the official money of Canada until the 1850s, but most provinces had established their own currency systems based on the Spanish and American dollars. Local tokens were made for small change. In the English-speaking provinces, they were pennies and halfpennies. In French-speaking Quebec (Lower Canada), the tokens were denominated in sou.

Nova Scotia
penny token, 1824

Upper Canada
halfpenny token, 1833

Lower Canada
sou token, 1837

Lower Canada
two-sou token, 1837

BRITISH COLUMBIAN GOLD
In 1862, this gold 20-dollar piece was made in British Columbia from local gold.

The native Indians traded furs for more exotic goods with British and French settlers

PROVINCIAL COINS
From 1858, when the Province of Canada (Ontario and Quebec) introduced an official bronze cent, similar coins were introduced in the other provinces. The coin (left) is from Prince Edward Island (1871), the coin (centre), from Nova Scotia (1861), and the coin (right), from Newfoundland (1938). Cents were also issued for New Brunswick.

TEN CANADIAN DOLLARS
This 1906 note of the Montreal office of the Merchants Bank of Canada is denominated in dollars. The Currency Act of 1868 established the dollar as the currency of the Dominion of Canada.

Silver 50-cent coin

Dollar coin

Totem pole design

Bronze one-cent coin

"Beaver" five-cent coin

DOMINION COINS
The first coins of the Dominion of Canada, silver 50, 25, 10, and 5 cents, were issued in 1870. A bronze cent was also issued from 1876. The first dollar coin was not issued until 1935. More recent issues, like the "beaver" five-cent, introduced in 1937, have wildlife designs.

Royal Canadian "Mountie"

COMMEMORATIVE DOLLARS
The Royal Canadian Mint issues many commemorative coins. These dollars celebrate the centenaries of British Columbia, 1958, and the Royal Canadian Mounted Police, 1973.

Today's money

PLASTIC CHIP
Plastic one-dollar gambling token from Diamond Tooth Gertie's casino in Dawson City, Yukon.

1$

25c

10c

5c

1c

49

See pages 62–63

Australia and New Zealand

BRITISH POUNDS, SHILLINGS, AND PENCE arrived in Australia and New Zealand with the first British settlers but, because of the many trade ships calling in, Indian, Dutch, Spanish, and Portuguese coins were more common. In 1792, settlers at Sydney Cove found a form of money more to their taste when *The Hope*, an American merchantship, delivered a cargo of rum. This precious liquid circulated as money in New South Wales until replaced in 1813 by Spanish American silver dollars (p. 21), which circulated officially until 1829. Today's dollar currencies were introduced by Australia in 1966, and New Zealand in 1967, when both countries adopted a decimal currency system in place of pounds, shillings, and pence.

GOLD!
In 1851, gold was found in Australia. Gold dust was used as money until 1852 when ingots (above) were made in Adelaide, followed by coins (top right). Private "Kangaroo Office" gold coins (centre) were made in 1853 at Port Phillip, Melbourne. A mint was established in Sydney in 1853 to make sovereigns (right), and half-sovereigns.

THE GREAT GOLD RUSH
The discovery of gold in Australia led many prospectors to search for gold.

"HOLEY DOLLAR" AND "DUMP"
From 1813 until 1822, dollars with a hole were the official currency of New South Wales. The silver "dump" cut from the middle was also official money. The dollar was valued at five shillings, and the dump at 15 pence.

Thames Goldfields penny token, 1874

"Advance New Zealand" penny token, 1881

NEW ZEALAND NOTES AND TOKENS
Although British coins were the official currency of New Zealand, most of the money in use during the 19th century was locally issued copper tokens and notes like this one issued in 1857 by a British commercial bank. More than 140 different tokens like those above were also issued.

BANK OF QUEENSLAND, LIMITED.

TOOWOOMBA

THREE · THREE

N° 1725 · N° 1725

I Promise to pay the Bearer on Demand, the Sum of THREE POUNDS in Cash here.

Batho & C° London.

FOR THE BANK OF QUEENSLAND, LIMITED.

THREE

Ent.......... Acct. .... MANAGER.

BRISBANE.

Australia's flightless, swift-running bird, the emu

BARTER
When Europeans arrived in Australia and New Zealand, they swapped cloth and metal tools for food with the Aboriginal and Maori peoples.

AUSTRALIAN NOTES AND TOKENS
During the second half of the 19th century, banknotes and local trade tokens provided most of the money in Australia. The Bank of Queensland issued the three-pound note (above) from its Brisbane office in 1865. The copper tokens from Tasmania and Western Australia were struck in Melbourne.

Today's money: New Zealand

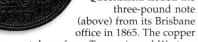

AUSTRALIAN COINS
In 1910, the Australians minted their own Australian Commonwealth coins. Silver florins (top), shillings (left), sixpences, and threepences were issued. From 1911, bronze pennies (right) and halfpennies joined them

NEW ZEALAND COINS
In 1933, New Zealanders also got their own coins. Silver half-crowns, florins (left), shillings (bottom left), sixpences, and threepences were issued. Bronze pennies and half-pennies (below) were made from 1940.

Today's money: Australia

This Maori "good luck" ornament (tiki), was featured on the bronze halfpenny from 1940 until 1965

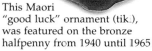

See pages 62–63

China and Japan

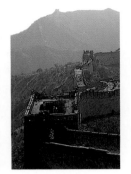

The Great Wall of China stretches for 2,400 km (1,500 miles)

THE MODERN CURRENCIES of both China and Japan developed from silver dollars (p. 21) introduced by European and American traders. They were exchanged for silk, tea, gold bars, porcelain, and rhubarb! Called "round coins", "yuan" in Chinese and "yen" in Japanese, the dollars took over from traditional currencies as the main form of money. China's coinage began in the 6th century B.C. (p. 11), and was later adopted by Japan. In China, silver and gold were only used as money by weight, but the Japanese developed their own precious metal coinage. Both countries played an important part in the development of paper money (pp. 12–13).

A Chinese money-changer

ANCIENT CHINA
Early Chinese coins were made of cast bronze in the shape of tools, like this hoe-coin (left) c. B.C. 300. This shape was inconvenient, so round coins with square holes (below) replaced them in B.C. 221, on the order of the first emperor of China, Qin Shihuangdi. Tool-shaped coins, like this knife-coin (right), were briefly re-issued by emperor Wang Mang (A.D. 7–23).

Inscription gives weight of coin: half an ounce

THE SHOGUN'S COIN
In 1626, the Shogun of Japan introduced new standard bronze coins. The inscription on them meant "generous, ever-lasting money".

BAMBOO MONEY
In 19th-century Shanghai, China, bamboo sticks were used as money instead of the heavy standard coins. This stick was worth 100 coins.

Holes for threading coins on strings

STANDARD COINS
In A.D. 621, the Chinese Tang Dynasty introduced a new standard bronze coin (top left) with a four-character inscription around its square hole. This design was used in China until the last issue in 1912. In A.D. 708, the same type of coin was introduced into Japan (left).

Inscription gives the weight (10 ounces), and the Mint Master's signature

MULTIPLE COIN
During a copper shortage in China, due to the capture of copper-mining areas by rebel forces, "multiple" coins were issued. This one (1854) was worth 1,000 standard coins.

"BIG PIECE" GOLD
This 1860 oban ("big piece") is typical of the gold coins of Japan during the Tokugawa Shogunate (1603–1868). Some Japanese clans issued their own coins, like this lead coin (above) from Kanagori.

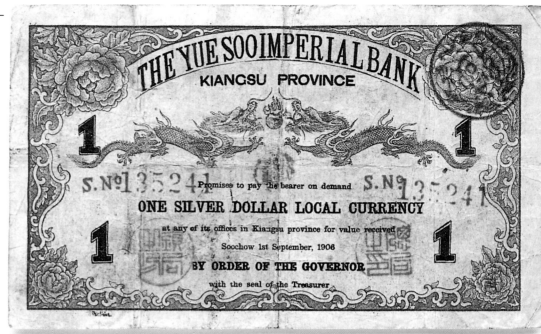

CHINESE DOLLARS

Many silver dollars were imported into China. In the 19th century, the Chinese began to make their own; firstly, unofficial local versions like this Taiwan dollar (1840s), then, from 1890, the Imperial Dragon dollars.

The figure on this Taiwan dollar is the Chinese god of long life

PAPER DRAGONS

As well as the silver dollars, the Chinese also used banknotes valued in dollars. This note was issued by the Imperial Bank of Jiangsu Province in 1906.

MEIJI EMPEROR

The Meiji Emperor, Mutsuhito, reigned in Japan from 1868–1912.

WORKERS OF THE WORLD UNITE!

So reads the slogan on this Chinese dollar issued by the Communist army in northwest China in 1934.

JAPANESE DOLLAR

The dollar influenced Japan to adopt this denomination for its own coinage. In 1870, the Meiji Emperor replaced the traditional Shogun coins with his own "dragon" dollar.

YUAN AND FEN

The Chinese called their dollar "yuan" (the round coin), and their cent "fen" (meaning a hundredth part). This two-fen note was issued by the Chinese People's Bank in 1953.

YEN AND SEN

The Japanese called their dollar "yen" (the round coin), and their cent, "sen" (the name of the traditional standard bronze coin). This ten-sen note of the Meiji Emperor was issued in 1872.

Today's money: China

10-fen foreign exchange certificate

10 fen (left) = 1 jiao (right)

5 fen   2 fen   1 fen

500 yen   10 yen

5 yen

Today's money: Japan

See pages 62–63

Africa

SOME OF THE EARLIEST RECORDS of the use of money come from Africa (pp. 8–9). The first African coins were issued about B.C. 500 by a Greek colony on the Libyan coast. Coinage soon became widespread from Egypt to Morocco, as Phoenician, local African, Roman, and Byzantine mints were established. From the 8th century onwards, Arab and Berber traders established caravan routes across the Sahara Desert to bring West African gold to the Islamic mints of North Africa, from where it was shipped into Europe to make coins. Further south, traditional means of payment, such as salt, cattle, cloth, and tools (pp. 8–9) continued to be the only form of money until coins and banknotes were introduced by European traders and settlers. In some areas, the traditional currencies have survived into the present century.

North

The emblem of Carthage was a horse, shown here as Pegasus

CARTHAGE
This large silver coin was made to pay troops during Carthage's (an ancient city in Tunisia) war with Rome (B.C. 264–241). The inscription is in Phoenician.

Arabic writing

BERBER GOLD
The Muwahhid Berber rulers of Morocco brought West African gold north across the Sahara. This Muwahhid coin was made in the 13th century.

FRENCH MOROCCO
This two-franc note was issued for use in the French Protectorate of Morocco during the Second World War. The French monetary system was used in Morocco from 1910 until 1960.

West

KISSI PENNY
Until the 1930s, pieces of iron wire, flattened at both ends, were used as money in Liberia and the neighbouring West African states. They were named after the Kissi people who made them.

PORTUGUESE AFRICA
This copper macuta was issued in Lisbon in 1762 for use in Angola. "Macuta" was the name of the local copper-bar money.

The Nigerian Ibo people preferred to use copper rings as money (p. 9)

LION DOLLAR
The British colony of Sierra Leone was established as a home for freed African slaves. A coinage of silver dollars was made for Sierra Leone in 1791.

LIBERIA
Liberia was also established as a home for freed slaves. Its American founders issued copper cents for the settlement in 1833. The design shows an African greeting freed slaves arriving home.

INDEPENDENCE
The Gold Coast was the first British colony to achieve independence; it became the new nation of Ghana in 1956. This coin shows the Founder of the State of Ghana, Kwame Nkrumah.

WEST AFRICAN MONETARY UNION
When the former French West African colonies achieved statehood in 1958, they joined together to issue a common currency that included this 100-franc note.

PHARAOH'S GOLD
The design on this coin of the Pharaoh Nectanebo II (B.C. 359–343) is made up from the Egyptian hieroglyphs meaning "good gold".

GREEK EGYPT
Alexander the Great established Greek rule in Egypt in B.C. 332. He is portrayed on this coin, made in about B.C. 310 by his successor in Egypt, Ptolemy I.

ROMAN EGYPT
After the death of Cleopatra, the Egyptian queen, the Romans ruled Egypt and issued their own coins there. This copper coin was issued by the emperor Nero (A.D. 54–68).

THALERS IN AFRICA
Before the Second World War, Ethiopian currency was based on imported Austrian silver thalers (p. 32). This note, issued during the reign of Emperor Haile Selassie, is denominated as two thalers in French and Ethiopian.

SWAHILI COIN
This copper coin was issued by the Swahili Sultan of Kilwa in Tanzania during the 15th century.

SUDANESE RING MONEY
This gold ring was used to make payments in Sudan during the late 19th century.

FATHER OF THE NATION
Many commemorative coins have been issued in African states to mark their independence. This 1966 gold coin portrays Jomo Kenyatta, "Father" of the Kenyan Nation.

French Madagascar: cut fragments of silver five-franc coin, about 1890

Portuguese Mozambique: gold 2.5 maticaes, 1851

Part of the design from a French Central African banknote

British Mombasa: rupee of the Imperial British East Africa Company (Kenya), 1888

French Madagascar: 10-centimes stamp money, 1916

German East Africa (Tanzania): gold 15-rupees, 1916

UNITED NATIONS COIN
This Zambian 50-ngwee coin was issued in 1969 to promote the work of the United Nations Food and Agriculture Organization. The design is an ear of maize, the staple diet of Zambia.

KRUGERRAND
The Republic of South Africa is one of the world's leading producers of gold, much of which is exported in the form of bullion coins known as krugerrands. Each gold krugerrand is made from 28 g (1 oz) of solid gold.

COLONIAL CURRENCIES
France, Germany, Britain, Italy, and Portugal all issued coins and notes for their East African colonies. They did not always introduce their own form of money, but matched the issues to those in use locally. Indian coins were widely used, so in 1888, the British issued a Mombasa rupee for use in Kenya. Rupees were also issued by the Germans in Tanganyika (now part of Tanzania), and by the Italians in Somalia. In Madagascar, the French introduced their own silver coins during the 19th century, but these were cut up by the local people, and the bits were valued in payments according to their weight.

See pages 62–63

Looking after money

MISERS HAVE NEVER been thought of kindly, but no one these days would question the wisdom of looking after money. Government saving schemes, banks, and building societies offer us the means of putting away our money for a "rainy day". Before the existence of savings banks, you could leave large sums of money with a merchant or goldsmith, but the only easy way of keeping your money safe was by burying or hiding it. It was this practice of hoarding money that created the image of the miser. At home, we often use a "piggy bank" to keep our savings safe.

BURIED TREASURE
This hoard of 17th-century Persian silver coins, hidden in a small, blue-glazed pot, was discovered in 1960.

LEATHER PURSE
This purse and the gold and silver coins it contains were left at a British court in the early 18th century. The money was saved over a long period of time: some of the coins were more than 150 years old.

PLASTIC "PURSES"
Keeping loose change in your pocket can be a nuisance. These two gadgets keep coins in place, and are both designed to hold British one-pound coins.

Most people these days pay their savings into a bank for safe-keeping

English oak tree emblem appeared on the back of British pound coins during 1987

Ring for closing the purse

Opening for coins

Slot for coins

METAL MONEY BOX
Lose the key to this small metal safe and you will never get your money out! The coins go into a self-sealing slot, and the notes into a curved slot on the other end. Serious savers would resist the temptation to spend their savings by leaving the key at the bank. In this way, they could only empty it into their bank savings account.

DRESS PURSE
The 19th-century dress purse above was designed to be carried on a belt, as you can see in this picture. Coins in each end would keep the purse balanced. The opening for the purse was a slit in the middle that was closed by moving the rings towards each end. However, these purses were not pick-pocket proof!

EAGLE AND CHICKS MONEY BOX
Novelty money boxes were very popular in 19th-century America. This example is operated by placing a coin in the eagle's beak. A handle pushes the eagle forward to "feed" its chicks and the coin falls into a slot at their feet.

Handle to push eagle forward

Coins were put in and taken out here

Mid-19th century British pottery pig

MONEY-PIG
The most popular form for money boxes is a pottery pig, but the reason for this preference is not known. In Europe, the earliest examples are 17th-century German "piggy banks", but earlier examples have been reported from 14th-century Indonesia. The pottery pigs usually have to be broken in order to get the money out.

SOCK PURSE
This woven cotton, sock-shaped purse from South America was also made to be worn on a belt. The long end was tucked into the belt and then pulled up to close the hole. When its wearer wanted to take coins out, he pulled it down far enough to open the hole.

TAMMANY BANK
This American novelty money box, made in 1873, has a political message. The seated figure is William "Boss" Tweed, a corrupt American politician who had his headquarters in Tammany Hall, New York. Every time you put a coin in his hand he drops it straight into his pocket!

William "Boss" Tweed sold political favours and defrauded New York City of at least 30 million dollars

Cheques and plastic

Although we normally think of money as the coins and notes in our pockets, most of today's money cannot be put in a pocket, or even be touched, because it exists only as electronic data held in bank and business computers. Some will be changed into cash before it is used, but most of it will be paid out into another computer. Before computers were invented, money was held in written records, and payments were made by written instructions, usually on printed forms called cheques. However, during the last few decades, plastic cards, some with built-in "computers", have begun to replace them.

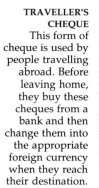

CHINESE BILL OF EXCHANGE
500 ounces of silver had to be paid out on the order of this bill issued in 1928 by the Yi-qing-xiang Bank of Hankou, central China.

AMERICAN CHEQUE
This cheque instructs a bank to pay 600 dollars to a Mr. John Negus, or to anyone to whom he gave the cheque, i.e. the Bearer.

TRAVELLER'S CHEQUE
This form of cheque is used by people travelling abroad. Before leaving home, they buy these cheques from a bank and then change them into the appropriate foreign currency when they reach their destination.

MONEY ORDER
A French sweet shop used this money order to pay a supplier 13 francs, 20 centimes for goods received. The stamp in the corner shows that the five-centimes tax on money orders has been paid.

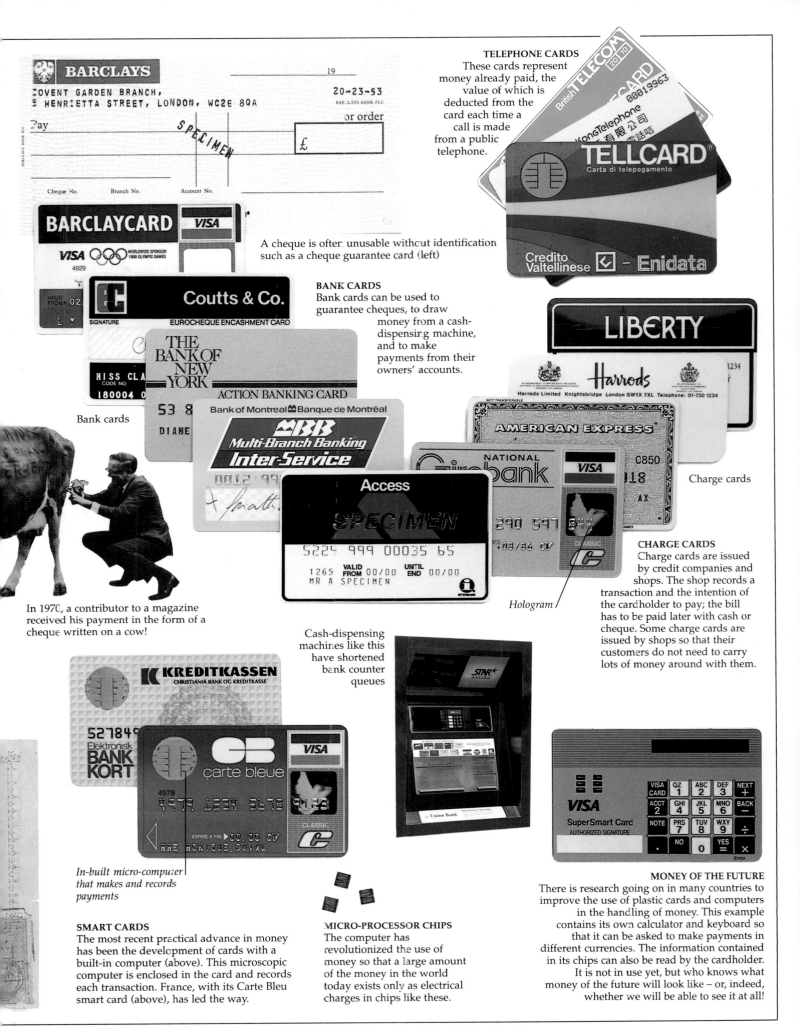

BARCLAYS

COVENT GARDEN BRANCH,
5 HENRIETTA STREET, LONDON, WC2E 8QA

19

20-23-53

BARCLAYS BANK PLC

Pay _____ SPECIMEN _____ or order

£ _____

Cheque No.   Branch No.   Account No.

A cheque is often unusable without identification such as a cheque guarantee card (left)

Bank cards

In 1970, a contributor to a magazine received his payment in the form of a cheque written on a cow!

TELEPHONE CARDS
These cards represent money already paid, the value of which is deducted from the card each time a call is made from a public telephone.

BANK CARDS
Bank cards can be used to guarantee cheques, to draw money from a cash-dispensing machine, and to make payments from their owners' accounts.

Cash-dispensing machines like this have shortened bank counter queues

Hologram

Charge cards

CHARGE CARDS
Charge cards are issued by credit companies and shops. The shop records a transaction and the intention of the cardholder to pay; the bill has to be paid later with cash or cheque. Some charge cards are issued by shops so that their customers do not need to carry lots of money around with them.

In-built micro-computer that makes and records payments

SMART CARDS
The most recent practical advance in money has been the development of cards with a built-in computer (above). This microscopic computer is enclosed in the card and records each transaction. France, with its Carte Bleu smart card (above), has led the way.

MICRO-PROCESSOR CHIPS
The computer has revolutionized the use of money so that a large amount of the money in the world today exists only as electrical charges in chips like these.

MONEY OF THE FUTURE
There is research going on in many countries to improve the use of plastic cards and computers in the handling of money. This example contains its own calculator and keyboard so that it can be asked to make payments in different currencies. The information contained in its chips can also be read by the cardholder. It is not in use yet, but who knows what money of the future will look like – or, indeed, whether we will be able to see it at all!

Collecting coins

THE DESIGNS AND INSCRIPTIONS on coins provide a fascinating view of the world's history. They reveal many things about the emperors, kings, and queens who issued them, as well as the traders and ordinary people who used them. Anyone can make their own collection, and one of the most interesting ways is by theme; collections featuring horses, boats, trees, and birds are shown here. The gold coins are all old and very expensive, but the coins in the plastic tray are all easy to obtain and could be bought with pocket money.

A soft toothbrush will not damage your coins

Methylated spirits

METHYLATED SPIRITS
The best way to clean coins is to rub them with methylated spirits on cotton wool. This will remove most of the grease and surface dirt.

Cotton wool balls

A cocktail stick will get most bits of dirt off without scratching, and a pen lid is good for getting coins out of the tray

SAVED FOR POSTERITY
Many of the coins now owned by collectors were once buried for safety. Luckily for the collectors, their owners were unable, or forgot, to recover them.

PAPER ENVELOPES
Because paper envelopes do not contain any acid, which causes corrosion, they will not damage your coins. Another advantage is that you can make notes on the front of them.

LOOKING AFTER YOUR COINS
Because old coins have been handled by lots of people, and perhaps even spent time buried in the ground, they are often very dirty. Clean them with methylated spirits, soap, or detergent first, and dry them thoroughly. If the dirt is stubborn, use a soft toothbrush or a piece of soft wood. If that does not work, seek advice from an experienced coin collector. The important thing is to experiment with cleaning coins that do not matter before you start on your star specimens!

A metal point can be used with caution

A magnifying glass is essential for looking at the fine details of coin designs

What not to do!

Keeping your coins clean and safely stored will make them nicer to look at and safe from corrosion. There are several things you should never do to your coins. Never use metal polish or a wire brush to clean coins – you will clean the designs right off them! Never store your coins in plastic envelopes; they may look nice when they are new, but after a while they go sticky and will ruin your coins. Never put your sticky fingers anywhere near coins, as this makes them dirty.

Sticky fingers have made this coin dirty

Never use plastic envelopes; they go sticky and may cause corrosion

A plastic envelope caused the green corrosion on this coin

RECORD YOUR COINS

You can make a catalogue of your own collection. A Japanese collector made this notebook record of his collection of Chinese and Japanese coins in 1812. He drew pictures of each coin and wrote down brief descriptions of them. Two examples of the coins he had are sitting on the book.

This 18th-century red leather tray was owned by a British nobleman

Gold-leaf decoration

A metal or plastic ring will help you hold the paper firmly

You can use rubbing wax instead of a pencil

A soft-leaded pencil will give a good result

COIN RUBBINGS

A useful and fun way to record your coins is by making rubbings of them; you only need a pencil and paper. Put your coin on a firm surface, put the paper over it, hold the paper down, and rub the pencil lead on the paper over the coin. An image of the coin will appear.

COIN TRAYS

Plastic or mahogany wood trays are best for storing old precious metal coins. Do not use any other wood, or cardboard, as these will cause corrosion. The coins in the leather tray are the sort of coins that would have been owned by a wealthy person. Leather trays should not be used for storing modern non-precious metal coins, as the leather causes these to corrode. The coins in the plastic tray are more recent, and could be bought with pocket money.

Studying coin details can be absorbing!

Money of the world

B<small>ANKNOTES AND COINS</small> are the everyday form of money throughout the world, but this does not mean that money is the same everywhere. Each country has its own notes and coins, and usually forbids the use of other countries' money within its own territory. This makes it awkward for travellers and traders who have to change their money into the local currency. This list gives some examples of the notes and coins now being issued by different countries. They are arranged geographically, working from the northwest of each continent to the southeast.

AMERICA

Canada
Dollar [$] (100 Cents)
Notes: 1,000; 500; 100; 50; 20; 10; 5; 2; 1 dollar
Coins: 1 dollar; 25; 10; 5; 1 cent

United States of America
Dollar [$] (100 Cents)
Notes: 1000; 500; 100; 50; 20; 10; 5; 2; 1 dollar
Coins: 25; 10; 5; 1 cent

Mexico
Peso
Notes: 50,000; 20,000; 10,000; 5,000; 2,000; 1,000; 500 peso
Coins: 500; 200; 100; 50; 20; 10; 5; 1 peso

Cuba
Peso (100 Centavos)
Notes: 100; 50; 20; 10; 5; 3; 1 peso
Coins: 1 peso; 20; 10; 5; 2; 1 centavo

Jamaica
Dollar [$] (100 Cents)
Notes: 100; 20; 10; 5; 2; 1 dollar
Coins: 1 dollar; 50; 25; 20; 10; 5; 1 cent

Ecuador
Sucre [S/]
Notes: 1,000; 500; 100; 50; 20; 10; 5 sucre
Coins: 1 sucre

Peru
Inti (100 Centimos)
Notes: 500; 200; 100; 50; 10; 5; 1 inti
Coins: 1 inti; 50; 10; 5 centimos

Brazil
Cruzado [Cz $] (100 Centavos)
Notes: 5,000; 1,000; 500; 100; 50; 10 cruzado
Coins: 50; 10; 5; 1 cruzado; 50; 20; 10 centavos

Chile
Peso
Notes: 5,000; 1,000; 500; 100 peso
Coins: 100; 50; 10; 5; 1 peso

Argentina
Australes (100 Centavos)
Notes: 100; 50; 10; 5; 1 australes
Coins: 50; 10; 5; 1; 1/2 centavo

EUROPE

Iceland
Króna (100 Aurar)
Notes: 1,000; 500; 100; 50; 10 króna
Coins: 10; 5; 1 króna; 50; 10; 5 aurar

Ireland
Pound/Punt [£] (100 Pence)
Notes: 100; 50; 20; 10; 5; 1 pound
Coins: 50; 20; 10; 5; 2; 1 pence

United Kingdom
Pound [£] (100 Pence)
Notes: 50; 20; 10; 5 pound
Coins: 1 pound; 50; 20; 10; 5; 2; 1 pence
England, Scotland, Northern Ireland, Wales, the Isle of Man, and the Channel Islands now use a monetary system based on the pound sterling divided into 100 pennies (pp. 46–47).

Denmark
Krone (100 Øre)
Notes: 1,000; 500; 100; 50; 20 krone
Coins: 20; 10; 5; 2; 1 krone; 50; 25 øre

Norway
Krone (100 Øre)
Notes: 1,000; 500; 100; 50 krone
Coins: 10; 5; 1 krone; 50; 25 øre
(New 1,000 kr note in 1990. New 500 kr note in 1991)

Sweden
Krona (100 Öre)
Notes: 10,000; 1,000; 500; 100; 50; 10 krona
Coins: 10; 5; 1 krona; 50; 10 öre

Finland
Markka (100 Pennia)
Notes: 1,000; 500; 100; 50; 10 markka
Coins: 10; 5; 1 markka; 50; 20; 10; 5; 1 penni
(New 10 and 50 penniä coins in 1990)

France
Franc [F] (100 Centimes)
Notes: 500; 200; 100; 50; 20 franc
Coins: 10; 5; 2; 1 franc; 50; 20; 10; 5 centimes

Belgium
Franc [BFr]
Notes: 5,000; 1,000; 500; 100 franc
Coins: 50; 20; 10; 5; 1 franc

Luxembourg
Franc [F]
Notes: 5,000; 1,000; 500; 100; 50; 20 franc
Coins: 10; 5; 1 franc
(Belgian franc is also legal tender)

Netherlands
Gulden (100 Cents)
Notes: 1,000; 250; 100; 50; 25; 10; 5 gulden
Coins: 5; 2.5; 1 gulden; 25; 10; 5 cents

German Federal Republic
Deutsch Mark [DM] (100 Pfennigs)
Notes: 1,000; 500; 100; 50; 20; 10 deutsch mark
Coins: 5; 2; 1 mark; 50; 10; 5; 2; 1 pfennig

German Democratic Republic
Mark [M] (100 Pfennigs)
Notes: 500; 100; 50; 20; 10; 5 mark
Coins: 20; 10; 5; 2; 1 mark; 50; 20; 10; 5; 1 pfennig

Switzerland
Frank/Franc (100 Rappen/Centimes)
Notes: 1,000; 500; 100; 50; 20; 10 franken
Coins: 5; 2; 1 frank; 50; 20; 10; 5 rappen

Austria
Schilling [S] (100 Groschen)
Notes: 5,000; 1,000; 500; 100; 50; 20 schilling
Coins: 20; 10; 5; 1 schilling; 50; 10 groschen

Czechoslovakia
Koruna (100 Haléru)
Notes: 1,000; 500; 100; 50; 20; 10 koruna
Coins: 5; 2; 1 koruna; 50; 20; 10; 5 haléru

U.S.S.R.
Rouble (100 Kopeks)
Notes: 100; 50; 25; 10; 5; 3; 1 rouble
Coins: 1 rouble; 50; 20; 15; 10; 5; 3; 2; 1 kopek

Poland
Zloty (100 Groszy)
Notes: 20,000; 10,000; 5,000; 2,000; 1,000; 500; 200; 100; 50 zloty
Coins: 20; 10; 5; 2; 1 zloty; 50, 20; 10 groszy

Portugal
Escudo (100 Centavos)
Notes: 5,000; 1,000; 500; 100 escudo
Coins: 50; 25; 20; 10; 5; 2.5; 1 escudo; 50 centavos

Spain
Peseta
Notes: 5,000; 2,000; 1,000; 500; 200; 100 peseta
Coins: 200; 100; 50; 25; 10; 5; 2; 1 peseta

Italy
Lira [L]
Notes: 100,000; 50,000; 20,000; 10,000; 5,000; 2,000; 1,000 lira
Coins: 500; 200; 100; 50; 20; 10 lira

Yugoslavia
Dinar
Notes: 20,000; 10,000; 5,000; 1,000; 500; 100; 50; 20; 10; 5 dinar
Coins: 100; 50; 20; 10; 5; 2; 1 dinar

Hungary
Forint (100 Fillér)
Notes: 1,000; 500; 100; 50; 20; 10 forint
Coins: 20; 10; 5; 2; 1 forint; 50; 20; 10 fillér

Greece
Drachma (100 Lepta)
Notes: 5,000; 1,000; 500; 100; 50 drachma
Coins: 50; 20; 10; 5; 2; 1 drachma; 50 lepton

Cyprus
Pound [£] (100 Cents)
Notes: 10; 5; 1 pound; 50 cents
Coins: 20; 10; 5; 2; 1; 1/2 cent

AFRICA

Morocco
Dirham [DH] (100 Centimes)
Notes: 100; 50; 10; 5 dirham
Coins: 5; 1 dirham; 50; 20; 10; 5 centimes

Algeria
Dinar [DA] (100 Centimes)
Notes: 200; 100; 50; 20; 10 dinar
Coins: 10; 5; 1 dinar; 50; 10; 5 centimes

Egypt
Pound [E£] (100 Piastres)
Notes: 100; 50; 20; 10; 5; 1 pound; 50; 25 piastres
Coins: 5; 1 pound; 20; 10; 5; 2; 1 piastre

Sudan
Pound [£S] (100 Piastres; 1,000 Millièmes)
Notes: 50; 20; 10; 5; 1 pound; 50; 25 piastres
Coins: 50; 10; 5; 2 piastres; 10; 5; 2; 1 millième

Ethiopia
Birr (100 Cents)
Notes: 100; 50; 10; 5; 1 birr
Coins: 50; 25; 10; 5; 1 cent

Nigeria
Naira (100 Kobo)
Notes: 20; 10; 5; 1 naira; 50 kobo
Coins: 25; 10; 5; 1; 1/2 kobo

Kenya
Shilling [Sh] (100 Cents)
Notes: 200; 100; 50; 20; 10 shilling
Coins: 5; 1 shilling; 50; 10; 5 cents

Zambia
Kwacha [K] (100 Ngwee)
Notes: 20; 10; 5; 2; 1 kwacha
Coins: 50; 20; 10; 5; 2; 1 ngwee

Botswana
Pula (100 Thebe)
Notes: 20; 10; 5; 2; 1 pula
Coins: 1 pula; 50; 25; 10; 5; 2; 1 thebe

Zimbabwe
Dollar [Z$] (100 Cents)
Notes: 20; 10; 5; 2; 1 dollar
Coins: 1 dollar; 50; 20; 10; 5; 1 cent

South Africa
Rand [R] (100 Cents)
Notes: 50; 20; 10; 5 rand
Coins: 2; 1 rand; 50; 20; 10; 5; 2; 1 cent

ASIA

Turkey
Lira [TL]
Notes: 10,000; 5,000; 1,000; 500; 100; 50 lira
Coins: 100; 50; 25; 20; 10; 5; 1 lira

Israel
New Shekel (100 Agorot)
Notes: 100; 50; 10; 5; 1 new shekel
Coins: 1 new shekel: 50; 10; 5; 1; 1/2 agorot

Iraq
Dinar (1,000 Fils)
Notes: 25; 10; 5; 1; 1/2; 1/4 dinar
Coins: 100; 50; 25; 10; 5; 1 fils

Saudi Arabia
Riyal (100 Halalah)
Notes: 500; 100; 50; 10; 5; 1 riyal
Coins: 100; 50; 25; 10; 5; 1 halalah

Iran
Rial (100 Dinars)
Notes: 10,000; 5,000; 2,000; 1,000; 500; 200; 100 rial
Coins: 50; 20; 10; 5; 2; 1 rial; 50 dinars

Pakistan
Rupee [Rs] (100 Paisa)
Notes: 500; 100; 50; 10; 5; 2; 1 rupee
Coins: 1 rupee; 50; 25; 10; 5; 1 paisa

India
Rupee [Rs] (100 Paise)
Notes: 1,000; 500; 100; 50; 20; 10; 5; 2; 1 rupee
Coins: 2; 1 rupee; 50; 25; 20 paise

Sri Lanka
Rupee [Rs] (100 Cents)
Notes: 1,000; 500; 100; 50; 20; 10; 5; 2 rupee
Coins: 5; 2; 1 rupee: 50; 25; 10; 5; 2; 1 cent

China
Yuan (10 Jiao; 100 Fen)
Notes: 10; 5; 2; 1 yuan; 5; 2; 1 jiao; (Foreign exchange notes also used)
Coins: 1 yuan; 5; 2; 1 jiao; 5; 2; 1 fen

Bangladesh
Taka (100 Poisha)
Notes: 500; 100; 50; 20; 10; 1 taka
Coins: 1 taka; 50; 25; 10; 5; 1 poisha

Burma
Kyat (100 Pyas)
Notes: 90; 45; 15; 10; 5; 1 kyat
Coins: 1 kyat; 50; 25; 10; 5; 1 pyas

Thailand
Baht (100 Satangs)
Notes: 500; 100; 50; 20; 10; 5 baht
Coins: 5; 2; 1 baht; 50; 25 satangs

Japan
Yen [¥]
Notes: 10,000; 5,000; 1,000; 500 yen
Coins: 500; 100; 50; 10; 5 yen

Singapore
Dollar [$] (100 Cents)
Notes: 10,000; 1,000; 500; 100; 50; 20; 10; 5; 1 dollar
Coins: 1 dollar; 50; 20; 10; 5; 1 cent

OCEANIA AND AUSTRALASIA

Australia
Dollar [$] (100 Cents)
Notes: 100; 50; 20; 10; 5; 2 dollar
Coins: 2; 1 dollar; 50; 20; 10; 5; 2; 1 cent

Papua New Guinea
Kina (100 Tooa)
Notes: 20; 10; 5; 2 kina
Coins: 1 kina; 20; 10; 5; 2; 1 tooa

Fiji
Dollar [$] (100 Cents)
Notes: 20; 10; 5; 2; 1 dollar
Coins: 20; 10; 5; 2; 1 cent

New Zealand
Dollar [$] (100 Cents)
Notes: 100; 50; 20; 10; 5; 2; 1 dollar
Coins: 50; 20; 10; 5; 2; 1 cent
(New $1 and $2 coins to replace notes in 1990)